Letters of
Francis A. Schaeffer

By *Francis A. Schaeffer*
   The God Who Is There
   Escape from Reason
   He Is There and He Is Not Silent
   Death in the City
   Pollution and the Death of Man
   The Church at the End of the 20th Century
   The Mark of the Christian
   The Church Before the Watching World
   True Spirituality
   Basic Bible Studies
   Genesis in Space and Time
   The New Super-Spirituality
   Back to Freedom and Dignity
   Art and the Bible
   No Little People
   Two Contents, Two Realities
   Joshua and the Flow of Biblical History
   No Final Conflict
   How Should We Then Live?
   Whatever Happened to the Human Race?
      (with *C. Everett Koop*)
   A Christian Manifesto
   The Great Evangelical Disaster
   The Complete Works of Francis Schaeffer
      (including all the above titles in five volumes)
   Everybody Can Know (with *Edith Schaeffer*)
   Letters of Francis A. Schaeffer
      (edited with introductions by *Lane T. Dennis*)

Letters of Francis A. Schaeffer

Spiritual Reality
in the Personal Christian Life

Edited with Introductions by
Lane T. Dennis

CROSSWAY BOOKS • WESTCHESTER, ILLINOIS
A DIVISION OF GOOD NEWS PUBLISHERS

First printing, 1985

Cover design: The Cioni Artworks/Ray Cioni

Printed in the United States of America

Library of Congress Catalog Card Number 85-70473

ISBN 0-89107-361-2

Contents

"But to this one I will look,
to him who is humble and contrite of spirit,
and who trembles at My Word."
(Isaiah 66:2 NASB)

Introduction

In a letter to a young woman struggling with her faith, Francis Schaeffer once wrote: "The practical problem for us individually is to find a point at which we can begin to live moment by moment in spiritual reality, . . . [in] a restored relationship with the God who is there, . . . act[ing] in faith upon what we believe in our daily lives." This statement, I would suggest, is more than just the summary of one individual Christian's struggle; it describes something essential about the Christian life which every Christian must learn.

The Innermost Circle Is the Spiritual
Where do we begin in order to know a deep sense of spiritual reality in our daily lives as Christians? How can we know the living presence of the Holy Spirit day by day and moment by moment? And what does it mean to live on the basis of this reality in the midst of life today?

The purpose of this collection of letters is to answer these questions in the most practical and personal way. But in a larger sense, this was the underlying purpose of Dr. Schaeffer's whole ministry. For Schaeffer, the question of whether or not there is spiritual reality at the center of one's life is the most important question in life. Of course, as Schaeffer wrote in *True Spirituality,* "The first point which we must make is that it is impossible even to begin living the Christian life, or to know anything of true spirituality, before one is a Christian. And the only way to become a Christian is not by trying to live some sort of a Christian life, but rather by accepting Christ as Savior" (in *The Complete Works,* Vol. 3, p. 199).

Salvation through faith in Christ is the essential beginning. Yet this is only the *beginning;* and if we settle only for the beginning, we will know only a very small fragment of what spiritual reality truly is. As Schaeffer explains further:

[Salvation is a unity]—a single piece, and yet a flowing stream. I become a Christian *once for all* on the basis of the finished work of Christ through faith; that is *justification.* [But] the Christian life, *sanctification,* operates on the same basis, but *moment by moment.* There is the same base (Christ's work) and the same instrument (faith). The only difference is that one is once for all and the other is moment by moment. The whole unity of Biblical teaching stands solid at this place. If we try to live the Christian life in our own strength, we will have sorrow; but if we live in this way, we will not only serve the Lord, but in the place of sorrow He will be our song. That is the difference. The how of the Christian life is the power of the crucified and risen Lord, through the agency of the indwelling Holy Spirit, by faith *moment by moment* (*True Spirituality* in *The Complete Works,* Vol. 3, p. 273).

We begin to know spiritual reality, then, when we receive Christ through faith (justification); but we begin to experience spiritual reality on a day by day basis (sanctification) as we live in daily communion with God. True spirituality begins with a restored relationship with a loving God; but then as the Holy Spirit works in our life, and as we are conformed increasingly to the person of Christ, a transformation begins to take place in every area of life.

A helpful way to look at this, I would suggest, is to think of the Christian life in terms of concentric circles. At the center is our personal relationship to Jesus Christ. The next circle, then, is the area of personal life. And if there is spiritual reality at the center, then we will begin to see a transformation of this next circle—that is, we will begin to know the power of God and His healing presence in the area of our personal lives. Beyond this, we might think of the next circle in terms of our family and other personal relationships. And beyond this, we might think of the wider circles of culture, various academic disciplines, social life, and politics. As the spiritual reality at the center of our life becomes greater and greater, the power of God and His healing presence begins to transform wider and wider circles of our lives until, as Schaeffer wrote, "the whole of life and culture" are touched and transformed in some way as God's power and presence works through us.

When we look at the life of Francis Schaeffer, we can see that there is a sense in which his whole life followed this pattern of concentric circles. Schaeffer's first encounter with spiritual reality began with his conversion as a young man of eighteen. Yet there came a point much later when Schaeffer realized that something was deeply wrong. At this point, when Schaeffer was thirty-nine years old, he realized that his own spiritual life had grown cold and lacked reality, and that nothing in his life and ministry really mattered if there was not spiritual reality at the center of his personal life. Thus the pattern of concentric circles can be seen in Schaeffer's life—first with the reawakening of spiritual reality, then with the impact of this in his personal life, and then into wider and wider circles reaching out to the whole of life and culture. (It is interesting to look at the range of Schaeffer's interests, writing, and activities in terms of these concentric circles. What we find is a shift in emphasis as Schaeffer's activities embraced wider circles of life and culture, but at the same time there was a genuine continuity founded upon an unchanging spiritual reality at the center of his life.)

Organization of the Book

The letters included in this volume have been selected and arranged with this pattern in mind. They begin in Part One with the "Reawakening of Spiritual Reality" as this unfolds in Schaeffer's own life. Part Two looks at how spiritual reality relates to the next circle, which I have called daily living. Part Three looks at the wider circle of spiritual reality in relation to

marriage, family, and sexual relations. At the same time I have
consciously chosen not to include letters dealing primarily with
the wider circles of culture, academic disciplines, social and political issues, etc. For one thing it would not have been feasible
to have included these in one volume, but they are also areas of
Schaeffer's thought which are much more widely known through
his books and films. The focus of this volume, then, has been
consciously limited to the priority of spiritual reality as the essential basis of every Christian's life, and how this relates to daily
living and the circle of marriage, family, and sexual relations.

Notes on Part One
I have titled Part One "The Reawakening of Spiritual Reality."
Included in this section are a selection of Dr. Schaeffer's letters
covering a period of ten years, from 1951 through 1960. The
first letter was written shortly after Schaeffer began to experience
the reawakening of spiritual reality in his own personal life. The
section then unfolds, over the next ten years, showing how this
"reawakening" took root, grew, and eventually brought about a
complete transformation in Schaeffer's life. The closing paragraphs of the last letter in this section (written in 1960) refer
back to the experiences of 1951 which brought about Schaeffer's
complete spiritual transformation.

It is fitting for these letters to come at the beginning of the
book, for through them we come to understand the whole basis
for Schaeffer's work—namely, that without spiritual reality in a
moment by moment relationship with Jesus Christ one can do
nothing of ultimate value in life. For Schaeffer the spiritual is
the center, which then reaches out to touch wider and wider
circles of life. Part One, then, shows the basis of spiritual reality
in Schaeffer's own personal experience.

In these letters we see a remarkable picture emerging. It is
the picture of a man who begins to see that, although he is a
Christian, he has somehow drifted away from the beauty and joy
he had known when he "first saw the face of the Lord," until he

realized there was a deadening lack of spiritual reality in his own life.

But I would suggest that this is much more than just another interesting example of spiritual reawakening. What we find here is a model from which every Christian can learn something profound about true spirituality, and which indeed provides the basic outlines of how the Spirit of God moves in true revival on the corporate level of the church and even in nations, as well as in personal life. In other words, here we find principles and patterns essential to every Christian if he or she is to know true spirituality and the beauty of a moment by moment relationship with the God of the universe and their personal Savior. And if these principles and patterns are followed—if even only a *few* Christians do begin to practice the holiness and love of God on a moment by moment basis—Schaeffer believed that the Holy Spirit would move in a mighty way throughout the church. (See Part One, letter dated August 8, 1955.) In this we are reminded of the early church Fathers' conviction and the conviction of C. S. Lewis "that holiness is actually to be practiced by the Christian and . . . that if only ten percent of the world's population had holiness the rest of the people would be converted quickly" (from the introduction to *C. S. Lewis: Letters to an American Lady,* edited by Clyde S. Kilby [Grand Rapids, Mich.: Eerdmans, 1967], p. 7).

The first letter begins shortly after Dr. Schaeffer began to realize that something was wrong in his own life. In the introduction to his book *True Spirituality* Schaeffer gives a brief description of how he experienced this. Schaeffer writes that in 1951,

> I faced a spiritual crisis. . . . I had become a Christian from agnosticism many years ago. After that I had become a pastor for ten years in the United States, and then for several years my wife Edith and I had been working in Europe. During this time [1948-1951] I felt a strong burden to stand for the historical Christian position, and for the purity of the visible church.

Gradually, however, a problem came to me—the problem of reality. This has two parts: first, it seemed to me that among many of those who held the orthodox position, one saw little reality in the things that the Bible so clearly says should be the result of Christianity. Second, it gradually grew on me that my reality was less than it had been in the early days after I had become a Christian. I realized that in honesty I had to go back and rethink my whole position.

We were living in Champéry [Switzerland] at the time [the early months of 1951], and I told Edith that for the sake of honesty I had to go all the way back to my agnosticism and think through the whole matter. I'm sure that this was a difficult time for her, and I'm sure that she prayed much for me in those days. I walked in the mountains when it was clear, and when it was rainy I walked backward and forward in the hayloft of the old chalet in which we lived. I walked, prayed, and thought through what the Scriptures taught, as well as reviewing my own reasons for being a Christian.

As I rethought my reasons for being a Christian, I saw again that there were totally sufficient reasons to know that the infinite-personal God does exist and that Christianity is true. In going further, I saw something else which made a profound difference in my life. I searched through what the Bible said concerning reality as a Christian. Gradually I saw that the problem was that with all the teaching I had received after I was a Christian, I had heard little about what the Bible says about the meaning of the finished work of Christ for our present lives. Gradually the sun came out and the song came. Interestingly enough, although I had written no poetry for many years, in that time of joy and song I found poetry beginning to flow again—poetry of certainty, an affirmation of life, thanksgiving, and praise. Admittedly, as poetry it is very poor, but it expressed a song in my heart which was wonderful to me.

This was and is a real basis of L'Abri. Teaching the historic Christian answers, and giving honest answers to honest questions are crucial, but it was out of these struggles that the reality came, and without which a work like L'Abri would not have been possible. I, and we, can only be thankful. (In *The Complete Works*, pp. 195, 196)

The letters included in this section are not intended to focus upon the people and the events which lie as a background to the reawakening of spiritual reality in Dr. Schaeffer's life. It was in fact very important to Schaeffer that the specific persons involved in these events *should not* be revealed, so that their personal privacy would not be violated. Equally important, however, it would be all too easy for us to become so caught up in condemning the failures of others that we may self-righteously overlook the need for spiritual reawakening in our own lives. Thus, in accord with Schaeffer's own wishes, we have included no "sensational" letters which would give personal details about the bitter conflict which Schaeffer was swept into. In fact, most of the letters pertaining to this controversy no longer exist, for as part of his own spiritual reawakening Schaeffer apparently burned most of these in 1955 as a kind of symbolic break with his own past and in repentance over something which he came to see had been deeply wrong.

Yet it is important for readers to have at least some understanding of the general background so that the spiritual principles learned by Schaeffer may be applied more easily to their own lives. All we really need to know is that Schaeffer was a leader in the "separated movement"—that is, a leader among those who had left the mainline denominations (which had become dominated by "theological liberalism" or "modernism"); in other words, he was a leader among those who stressed historic Christian orthodoxy and the complete authority and inerrancy of the Bible.

Schaeffer never abandoned his commitment to the principles of "the purity of the visible church," but by 1951 he realized that there was something profoundly wrong within the separated movement. Basically this problem was the total lack of love among many of the movement's leaders—so much so that it became filled with hatred, bitterness, and brutal tactics which were directed not only against their modernistic opponents but increasingly against one another *within* the separated movement. Again it must be stressed that Schaeffer never became a modernist, nor did he abandon the positive principles which led Christians to "separate" from churches which did not really affirm historic Christian orthodoxy.

But the error Schaeffer discovered was grave indeed. It nearly destroyed his own faith, while it made shipwreck of the lives of many and of the separated movement as a whole. Schaeffer eventually came to the place where he realized that this was so profoundly wrong that he described it as "counterfeit Christianity" and a "heresy of practice."

It is against this background, then, that the letters included in Part One may be understood. But there is something much more significant here. It is the pilgrimage of one of the spiritual giants of this century—of how, at the age of thirty-nine, he came to a spiritual crisis in his own life; how he came to terms with spiritual deadness and spiritual pride; how he learned to bring everything under the blood of Christ; how he sought to live moment by moment in the presence of the Lord; how he stepped out in faith under the impossible circumstances; how he eventually came to see, as he says in one letter, "a little of the blazing glory of God."

Perhaps the most important insight which we find in these letters is Schaeffer's eventual realization that *nothing* matters in life unless there is spiritual reality in one's own personal life. The innermost circle, Schaeffer writes, is the spiritual. And if there is not reality at the center—if we do not know Jesus Christ in a personal way, living in the reality and the power of His presence—then nothing else really matters.

In reading these letters we see the unfolding of spiritual reality in Schaeffer's own life. And in this unfolding we encounter something of our own spiritual crisis—our frailty, our failure, our sin—and we are driven to the cross of our Lord and Savior.

Notes on Part Two

Part Two, really, is the application of what spiritual reality means in the wider circle of personal daily living. Here we find letters dealing with the central concerns of daily life—finding forgiveness for sin; coping with fear, depression, sickness, and death; turning failure into something of beauty; living moment by moment in the power and presence of the Holy Spirit; prayer and the daily walk. With the exception of two letters from 1953, all of the letters in this section were written between 1961 and 1982—after Schaeffer had come to terms with the meaning of spiritual reality in his own personal life.

The letters in this part look at the reality of the human condition with a rare sense of honesty. Most of us carry on our lives behind a fragile veneer of romantic optimism. For many of those to whom Dr. Schaeffer writes in this section, however, the veneer has been stripped away. They have written to share their deepest spiritual needs and are reaching out for help in a way that most of us are seldom willing to do. In Schaeffer's responses he often mentions how deeply he is moved by their need— sometimes bringing him to tears, while often lifting them up in prayer.

But in these letters we are reminded of our own frailty and our own need, for often our veneer is also cracking. And when we are honest with ourselves, we too are broken people, deeply affected by the Fall and in need of God's saving grace. Even though we may not feel them acutely at this moment, the realities of life in a fallen world—depression, tragedy, sickness, death—will touch every one of us. The only answer for facing these realities is to have one's life grounded in the reality of Him who has conquered sin and death. Thus Schaeffer affirms repeatedly that as Christians we do know the infinite-personal God who is there; we know that the victory has been won on the cross, and one day we will be made whole. And in this life we can begin to know a measure of wholeness, of substantial healing, of some small work of beauty, giving us a foretaste of the victory and glory which Christ has prepared for us.

Notes on Part Three
In Part Three the meaning of spiritual reality is extended to cover the circle of marriage, family, and sexual relations. Here

too we find a rare sense of honesty as Schaeffer writes concerning the most intimate areas of human life, including questions concerning fulfillment in marriage, divorce, sexual relations before marriage, homosexuality, lesbianism, male-female roles, restoring a broken marriage, and related topics. As with Part Two, all but a few letters in this part come from the 1960s, seventies, and early eighties after the period of spiritual reawakening which Schaeffer went through in the early 1950s.

Perhaps the single theme which comes through most clearly in this section is Schaeffer's way of "speaking the truth in love." Here we find a rare combination of an uncompromising commitment to the absolutes revealed in God's Word, the rejection of any form of cultural morality which cannot be supported by Scripture, and a care and compassion for others which often brought Schaeffer to tears.

Editing and Background

Shortly before his death, Dr. Schaeffer commented that the focus of the letters should not be upon himself, but upon "subjects dealt with in a practical and often pastoral way—not as an academic discussion—hoping to be of real help to the people who read them." His goal was that the letters might speak to the general reader in a clear and personal way, providing practical advice and spiritual insight.

This goal was foremost in my mind throughout the editing and selection. But at the same time Schaeffer's presence, of course, could not be eliminated from the letters. Because of this, those who read these letters will have the happy opportunity to know, at least in some small way, this other side of Schaeffer—as the man who would give hours of his personal time to open up his heart, and often pray and weep with those in need.

Schaeffer was also concerned that the personal identity of each person receiving his letters would not be revealed, and that the confidentiality of the letters would not be breached in any way. Thus only Schaeffer's replies have been included, and nothing from the original letters appears in the book. In addition to this, pseudonyms have been used in place of all personal names throughout the letters. (There are a few exceptions to this—for example, where Schaeffer mentions well-known figures such as classic Christian writers, including Amy Carmichael, F. B. Meyer, G. Campbell Morgan, and others, or liberal theologians, including Karl Barth and Emil Brunner.) Where certain details might give a clue to the identity of a person, these have either been changed or eliminated so that it would be impossible to identify the recipient of any of the letters included. Although Schaeffer did correspond with a number of prominent Christian leaders, none of these letters were included.

Most of the letters include a brief introduction describing the general situation which Schaeffer is addressing in his response. I tried to keep these as brief as possible—but still to provide a general frame of reference so that Schaeffer's reply could be understood clearly and applied when appropriate to the reader's own situation. At the same time, the reader should be cautioned not to try to apply the answers in Schaeffer's letters as simplistic formulas. The Letters need to be understood in relation to Schaeffer's thought as a whole, and in light of the Scriptures as a whole. But they also need to be read as personal responses to personal situations, and as such cannot be applied as a simple formula without consideration for one's own personal situation. (Again, it should be noted that the details contained in the introductions are not sufficient to identify the person receiving the letter and in some cases certain details have been altered to insure that this is impossible.)

I retained as much of each letter as seemed best. Some extraneous material was dropped, but in most cases openings, closings, and personal comments were retained since these help to give a sense of the personal interest which Schaeffer took in everyone to whom he wrote. Three dots (. . .) were used to indicate the omission of some material. Brackets ([]) were used to indicate material which was added for clarity. (See, further, the Appendix following the letters for complete details on how the editing was handled.)

Although the letters, for the most part, can be read and appreciated without previous background on the lives of Francis and Edith Schaeffer, some crucial details have been provided in the introductions to specific letters. Beyond this, it may be helpful to know a general outline of time frame (1948-1983) during which these letters were written. The Schaeffers moved to Switzerland with their three young daughters in 1948. Prior to this, Dr. Schaeffer had been a pastor in the Bible Presbyterian denomination during the ten preceding years. From 1948 through 1953 the Schaeffers were missionaries to Europe with their home in Switzerland under the Independent Board of Presbyterian Foreign Missions. Their work involved speaking, evangelism, and starting children's groups for Children for Christ. To a lesser extent, Dr. Schaeffer did organizational work for the International Council of Christian Churches, whose purpose was to bring fundamental churches around the world into fellowship and a loosely affiliated organization. Schaeffer's spiritual crisis reached its critical turning-point in the early months of 1951. The Schaeffers were on furlough in the U.S. in 1953-1954. In 1955 the Schaeffers resigned from the Independent Board to begin the work of L'Abri Fellowship in a step of total faith and dependence upon God to supply their needs. Dr. Schaeffer led L'Abri, along with Edith, up until shortly before his death in 1984. For clarification on these and other events it may be helpful, especially as the letters are being read, to refer to the brief chronology found on pages 25-28.*

A Place to Begin

In thinking back to the beginning of these introductory comments, we asked: Where do we begin in order to know a deep sense of spiritual reality in our daily lives? How can we know the living presence of the Holy Spirit, day by day and moment by moment? And what does it mean to live on the basis of this reality in the midst of life today? Many of us long for true spiritual reality in our own lives. I am sure that it would be the wish of Dr. Schaeffer, as well as my own wish, that this book might provide a place to begin for many—in the discovery of a deep sense of spiritual reality and a moment by moment relationship with our loving Lord.

In reading these letters each of us will find something of ourselves, our frailty, and our human need, but also something of what we might become as Christians and as human beings through the transforming presence of Jesus Christ in our own lives—as was so clearly the case in the life of Francis A. Schaeffer.

Lane T. Dennis
August 1985

*For further background on the Schaeffers' lives see Edith Schaeffer's two biographies *L'Abri* (Wheaton, Ill.: Tyndale House, 1969) and *The Tapestry* (Waco, Texas: Word Books, 1981). A full-scale biography of Francis Schaeffer, written by Harold Fickett, is scheduled for publication in 1986 by Crossway Books, Westchester, Ill. See also the popular treatment of Schaeffer by L. G. Parkhurst, *Francis Schaeffer: The Man and His Message* (Wheaton, Ill.: Tyndale House, 1985).

Table of Letters

Part One

The Reawakening of Spiritual Reality

Part Two

Spiritual Reality in Daily Living

Part Three

Spiritual Reality in Marriage, Family, and Sexual Relations

Chronology

1912   Francis August Schaeffer was born on January 30 in Germantown, Pennsylvania. He was the only child of Francis August Schaeffer III and Bessie Williamson Schaeffer.

1914   Edith Rachel Merritt Seville (Francis Schaeffer's future wife) was born in China on November 3. She was the fourth child of George Hugh Seville and Jessie Maude Merritt Seville.

1930   Schaeffer became a Christian at the age of eighteen after reading the Bible, beginning with Genesis, for about six months.

1932   Met his future wife on June 26 at the First Presbyterian Church of Germantown, Pennsylvania.

1935   Graduated from Hampden-Sydney College in June. Schaeffer was second in his senior class and graduated *magna cum laude*.

1935   Married Edith Seville on July 26.

1935   Entered Westminster Theological Seminary in September.

1937   The Schaeffers' first daughter, Priscilla, was born on June 18.

1938   Schaeffer graduated from Faith Theological Seminary, which he had helped to found after a split with Westminster in 1937.

1938   Ordained as the first pastor in the Bible Presbyterian denomination, and began serving as pastor of Covenant Presbyterian Church in Grove City, Pennsylvania.

1941   Elected moderator of the Great Lakes Presbytery of the Bible Presbyterian Church.

1941   Began serving as associate pastor of the Bible Presbyterian Church in Chester, Pennsylvania.

1941   The Schaeffers' second daughter, Susan, was born on May 28.

1943   Began serving as the pastor of the Bible Presbyterian Church in St. Louis, Missouri.

1945   The Schaeffers' third daughter, Deborah, was born on May 3.

1947   Traveled throughout Europe for three months to evaluate the state of the church in Europe as a representative of the Independent Board for Presbyterian Foreign Missions and as the American Secretary for the Foreign Relations Department of the American Council of Christian Churches.

1948   Moved to Lausanne, Switzerland with Edith and their three daughters to be missionaries to Europe. Their work primarily involved the Children for Christ ministry, and helping with the formation of the International Council of Christian Churches.

1949   Moved to Chalet des Frênes in the mountain village of Champéry, Switzerland.

1951   Went through a spiritual crisis in the winter months. During this time, Schaeffer recognized that something was deeply wrong and he carefully reconsidered his Christian commitment and the priorities in his life. Schaeffer emerged from this experience with a new certainty about his faith, a new emphasis on sanctification and the work of the Holy Spirit, and a new direction in his life which would unfold over the next four years.

1952   Francis August Schaeffer IV was born on August 3.

1953   Returned to the U.S. with family on furlough.

1953-   Traveled across the country speaking 346 times during 515
1954   days about the deeper spiritual life. During this time Schaeffer first presented the talks which grew out of his spiritual crisis and later became the basis for his book *True Spirituality.*

1954   Awarded honorary Doctor of Divinity degree in May by Highland College in Long Beach, California.

1954   Returned to Champéry, Switzerland in September. Franky Schaeffer contracted polio on the boat en route to Switzerland.

1955   Received notice from the Swiss government on February 14 that they must leave Switzerland permanently within six weeks.

1955 The Schaeffers moved into Chalet les Mélèzes in Huémoz, Switzerland on April 1 after receiving the money needed to purchase les Mélèzes through a series of miraculous circumstances.

1955 Resigned from the Independent Board for Presbyterian Foreign Missions on June 4, marking the informal beginning of L'Abri Fellowship.

1955- Francis Schaeffer, along with Edith, lead the work L'Abri as
1984 the primary focus of their lives, up until shortly before Dr. Schaeffer's death.

1958 English L'Abri is founded after Schaeffer gave lectures at Oxford and elsewhere in England.

1968 Published *The God Who Is There*, the first of his twenty-three books, based on lectures given at Wheaton College in 1965.

1971 Received honorary Doctor of Letters degree in June from Gordon College in Wenham, Massachusetts.

1974 Began work on the book and film for *How Should We Then Live?* with Franky Schaeffer.

1977 Began a twenty-two-city seminar and speaking tour in January for the film series *How Should We Then Live?*

1977 Helped to found the International Council on Biblical Inerrancy.

1977 Began work on the film series *Whatever Happened to the Human Race?* with C. Everett Koop and Franky Schaeffer.

1978 Diagnosed as having lymphoma cancer in October, at Mayo Clinic in Rochester, Minnesota.

1979 Began a national seminar and speaking tour in September for the film series *Whatever Happened to the Human Race?*

1979 The American headquarters of L'Abri was established in Rochester, Minnesota.

1982 Publication of *The Complete Works of Francis A. Schaeffer* in July.

1983 Received honorary Doctor of Laws degree from the Simon Greenleaf School of Law.

1983 Was flown in critical condition from Switzerland to Mayo Clinic in December.

1984 Went on a seminar tour to ten Christian colleges during March and April in connection with his last book *The Great Evangelical Disaster.*

1984 Died in his home in Rochester, Minnesota on May 15.

PART I
The Reawakening of Spiritual Reality

Missing the Woods For the Trees

[To a close friend in the U.S. who was a leader in higher education within the Bible Presbyterian denomination. The Schaeffers were especially close to Jeffrey and his wife, Hope, in the late 1940s and early 1950s. The excerpt below comes mostly from the end of a long letter dealing with personal interests and organizational matters in the "separate movement." Although Dr. Schaeffer added this to the end of his letter almost as an afterthought, it reflects the beginning of a basic change in Schaeffer's thinking which will eventually transform his life completely.

[This letter was written shortly after the "spiritual crisis" Schaeffer went through, in the early months of 1951. (See further Introduction, pages 7-19.) In this and the next few letters we see how Schaeffer's thinking gradually changes, until his life is totally transformed. In the *Sunday School Times* article, mentioned at the end of the letter, Schaeffer outlined, for the first time in print, his growing emphasis upon spiritual reality in daily life, the need for devotional literature, and the need for balance between the love and holiness of God. The article set off a major controversy in the "separated movement" and marked a watershed in the thinking and lives of the Schaeffers.]

14th April 1951   Chalet des Frênes
                             Champéry, Switzerland

Dear Jeffrey,

Thank you for your two letters. My, what a pleasure it was to hear from you at such length! . . . Edith's last letter will tell you of all the things the Lord has been doing for us. Really, in spite of the grippe, which Edith, Deborah, and Susan had, it has been a time of spiritual blessing. The children got over the grippe quickly, but it has left Edith rather weak. This was complicated by our having taken a trip this past week to speak in several Swiss cities for Children for Christ, and by the need of moving at the end of this month. . . .

I have had a rather interesting experience recently. (I notice that this letter is much too long already, but I am going to add this as I think it might be a lesson to you.) There really are many things about our [separated] movement which have made me increasingly unhappy. I do not think our movement is in the place where the Lord can bless it, as its basic principles would seem to indicate. Not that I think our separation is wrong—my time in Europe has convinced me that we are 1,000 percent right in this. But I do think that [certain ones among our men] have missed the woods for the trees.

I do not think we can throw everything we can lay our hands on [i.e., fight without any restraint] even against the World Council of Churches—let alone in dealing with those who differ from us in our own work—and then expect the Lord to bless our efforts. I think we have to be involved in the combat. But when we are fighting for the Lord, it has to be according to His rules, does it not? What I am saying is probably the same thing you have said . . . in the past, but from a little different viewpoint. Anyway, I never got any joy out of this contemplation, but only got down in the dumps. The more time I have with the Lord, the more discouraged I become about it.

Then over Easter, I went to Geneva to speak . . . at Hugh E. Alexander's Easter Conference. He is a Scotchman, spiritually born out of the Welsh revivals, and a man who has taken the best position of anyone in Switzerland; he is able to do a really big work. While there, the Lord really spoke to my heart. I had never heard anyone talk and sing about the combat the way those people did. And yet at the same time there was such a spiritual emphasis on the dependence upon the leading of the Holy Spirit, identification with Christ, the need of dying to serve the Lord, and so on and so on, that since being there I felt the burden lifted away. Not that I think the problem is less, but for the first time I see the basic answer. It is the thing for which I have been groping, I think. It is not less combat, but a balance between it and a real following the leading of the Holy Spirit— in short, a care that we do not minimize our personal spiritual lives.

I really feel lighter than I have for years. I do not know what this all means in my relationship to the movement, but I have come to this conclusion—that, God willing, I do not want to lose this joy I have before the Lord. There is nothing that would be worth getting back into the black humor I have been in.

Enclosed is a copy of an article I have just sent off to the *Sunday School Times.* I have been writing it for two years; it has meant more to me than any article I have ever written. I do not know if they will print it, but I am sure the Lord has a use for it somewhere.

May the Lord bless you. And let us spend a real time in prayer together that the Lord will show the balance between purity and love, which will give us a real joy in our Lord and then power in His service.

Your friend,
Francis A. Schaeffer

Quiet in the Presence of God

26th May 1951   Chalet Bijou
                                Champéry, Switzerland

Dear Jeffrey,

I have not heard from you since my last letter, but thought I would write you this short note. . . .

My mind is not at rest by any means about all the problems I raised in my last letter to you. I do think that our movement will never be what it could be under the Lord unless the leadership learns to be quiet in the presence of God. It does seem to me that there is a constant tendency to smooth over problems and to the loss not of the weak men, but the stronger ones—perhaps not the loss physically, but the loss as far as leadership is concerned.

I am more and more realizing that Scripturally none of us are ready for leadership until we come to the place before the Lord where we are really ready for His will—regardless of what it is—and therefore, of ourselves, we would prefer not to have the leadership, or at least be neutral concerning it. It is out of such stuff that true Christian leadership can come.

I have been thinking and thinking: can you think of any American who has written really deep devotional literature? And can you think of anyone in our separationist movement in America who has written devotional literature that really is deep in its contact with the heart? When you read Bonar, Murray, and so on, there is an impact that one never forgets. I wonder who among our men has written anything even looking in this direction.

May the Lord bless you. . . . By the way, the *Sunday School Times* has accepted the article of which I sent you a copy.

Please give our greetings to Hope.

Cordially yours in Christ,
Francis A. Schaeffer

God's Power Without Reservation

[To a fellow minister and friend who has just become the pastor of an independent fundamental church.]

October 26, 1951   Chalet Bijou
                                    Champéry, Switzerland

Dear Mike,

Thank you so much for your letter of September 13. . . . I appreciate what you say about your friendship in Christ towards me, and I wish to assure you that I feel exactly the same way towards you. . . .

[Concerning tensions you have been facing in your ministry], quite frankly, there have been questions developing in my own mind during these past years since I have been in Europe. We have been here over three years now. And although we have been exceedingly busy, at the same time it is not exactly the same kind of business that we have had previously. Sitting here in my study as I dictate this, I look out across the trees, over to a huge cliff and up the mountains to the rocky peaks of the *Dents du Midi*. Somehow there is a quietness here that lends a quietness to one's soul and thinking.

As I have thought perhaps more quietly than in previous days, it has seemed to me that in the past there has been a fallacy in my thinking. That fallacy is simply this: that insofar as we are so abundantly right (as we *are* concerning the Biblical position of separation), therefore it would certainly follow of a necessity that God's rich blessing would rest upon us as individuals and as a movement. I no longer believe this is so. For increasingly the realization has welled up in my own soul that although this principle [of separation] is of tremendous importance, nevertheless there are other principles in the Word of God which must be kept with equal fidelity if God's full blessing is to be upon us. . . .

What does all this mean to me? I am not sure, except that it brings me increasingly to my knees—to ask that the Holy Spirit may have His way in my life; that I may not think just of justification and then the glories of Heaven (with merely a battle for separation between). [But that I may also think of] all the wonders of the present aspect of my salvation, and that they may be real to me in my life and ministry. What a wonderful Lord we have, and how glorious it is to indeed have God as our Father, and to be united with Christ, and to be indwelt by the Holy Spirit. Oh, would to God that our ministry could be under His full direction, and in His power without reservation.

I hope these things are not troublesome to you. But in the light of your letter I thought that I should say them. May the Lord bless you. Edith and I send our greetings to Helen and to you as well as to your dear children. I will be waiting with expectancy to hear from you again.

May God bless you with every good thing.

Cordially yours in Christ,
Francis A. Schaeffer

Gradually My Thinking Has Changed

[Between Dr. Schaeffer's letter to Jeffrey of April 14, 1951 and this letter, the two had other warm exchanges of correspondence. Much of this dealt with the growing conflict and controversy within the "separated movement." Schaeffer replied here to a six-page letter from Jeffrey with his own long letter running seventeen pages, written first in longhand and later typed by Edith. A large part of the letter is included here since it is crucial in understanding the mistakes which Schaeffer believes he and "the movement" have made, and for seeing the growing sense of spiritual reality in Schaeffer's life.]

November 8, 1951   Chalet Bijou
                          Champéry, Switzerland

My dear Jeffrey,

I cannot tell you how much I appreciate your writing your recent long letter. Do not feel the compulsion to read this all at once. I am going to write it as the mood is upon me, and I do not know how long I will take to finish it.

Tonight it is rainy outside, but a little higher in the mountains the snow is falling again. The wood fire is crackling with a rich personality. The children are sleeping, and Edith is typing some things which she feels she must do. In short, it is quiet here—the quiet that only the mountains can give.

As I was walking home from the post office today, where I had gone to send off a great pile of letters and some packages, I was thinking of my answer to you. And as I walked I looked up at the Dents with their swirling mists so high above me. I thought how our dear Lord comes into more proper perspective in our thinking in such a place as this—for the higher the mountains, the more understandable is the glory of Him who made them and who holds them in His hand. But the other side is also true: man also comes into his proper place. As the Lord gains in greatness, in comparison to the mountains, so man diminishes.

As it is with space, it is also true of time. My letters from here go to so many countries, and in these last few years I have found friends in many of them. As I have learned the history of these lands, from those who tell the history from their hearts, time has come to mean something different to me than it ever did before, when time was measured only by the short scope of the hurrying clock or cold dates on a page of the history book. But as time falls into its proper place, again God seems to grow greater by comparison, and again it has the opposite effect on man. As the mountains shrink him down to size, so also does time.

Then too, time is getting clearer to me because more of it has passed me by. In a couple of months I'll be forty now, and as I look at Priscilla I realize indeed that time has been passing. If God will spare me, I will have more time yet ahead than has already passed me since I came to mature thinking. But it does not seem to stretch forever as it did even when I first came to Europe four years ago.

The three and a half years since I came to Europe have been the most profitable in my life, with only one possible competitor, my three years in seminary. But certainly (with that one possible exception) no period even three times as long has marked me so.

First, the things of which I spoke above—the rectifying process of space and time—have caused my view of the Lord to grow greater, and my view of man and his works and judgments to grow proportionately smaller.

Second, for the first time since I entered college I have had a chance to think. Not that we have not been busy here; we have been, but it is a bit different from the rush of college, seminary, and then ten years in the pastorate. Gradually my thinking has changed—I have realized that in many things previously I have been mistaken.

When I first found Christ through my Bible reading He was very real to me, and I yet remember the loving wonder of His closeness. And then came the struggle against the Old [Presbyterian] Church machine, and then against Westminster, and then against the N.A.E. [National Association of Evangelicals], and gradually "the [separatist] movement" loomed larger and larger. Do not misunderstand me: my experiences here have convinced me more than ever that each of these struggles was needed and right; but the correct perspective got mislaid in the process. And I tell you frankly, that though I realize I may be wrong, it seems to me that I was not alone in my mistake—that many are as deeply involved, or even more, than I have been. The "movement" grew in our thinking like the great bay tree until for me that wonderful closeness which I had felt to Him in previous days was lost. I wonder if that is not what happened to the Church of Ephesus in Revelation 2?

It seems to me all things became grist for the movement's mill. . . . And if things or people got in the way, they were to be blasted. The Presbyterian Church fight [in the early and mid-1930s] was a rough school of battle. First at unbelief, and then as time went on, at that which represented unbelief, the Federal Council [of Churches]. We threw everything which came to hand. And then as "the movement" grew, the N.A.E. stood in the way . . . and it seems to me we continued to throw everything we had at hand. Again, don't misunderstand me: from my experience here [in Europe] I am sure that we were correct in saying that the N.A.E. was wrong. But we could have remembered that, wrong though they are, they are for the most part brothers in Christ. . . .

But "the movement" rolls on, and now differences arise between us. Quickly the pattern repeats itself; the habit is too well learned. The movement is in jeopardy! So everything is thrown again [this time at one another within the movement]. . . . And who is wounded? We are and our Lord. . . .

I am sure "separation" is correct, but it is only one principle. There are others to be kept as well. The command to love should mean something. . . . [I am not suggesting that] I have learned to live in the light of Christ's command of love—first toward God, then the brethren, and then the lost. I know I have not. But I want to learn, and I know I must if I am to have that closeness to the Lord I wish to have, with its accompanying joy and spiritual power. . . .

. . . God willing, I will push and politick no more. . . . The mountains are too high, history is too long, and eternity is longer. God is too great, man is too small, there are many of God's dear children, and all around there are men going to Hell. And if one man and a small group of men do not approve of where I am and what I do, does it prove I've missed success? No; only one thing will determine that—whether *this day* I'm where the Lord of lords and King of kings wants me to be. To win as many as I can, to help strengthen the hands of those who fight unbelief in the historical setting in which they are placed, to know the reality of "the Lord is my song," and to be committed to the Holy Spirit—that is what I wish I could know to be the reality of each day as it closes.

Have I learned all this? No, but I would not exchange that portion of it which I have, by God's grace, for all the handclapping I have had when I have been on the top of the pile. I have been a poor learner, but I'm further on than I was three years ago and I like it.

Jeffrey, I've seen the Holy Spirit work in individual lives like I have never experienced before. It reminds me of what I've heard of the revivals of yesterday. It would not be counted for much—only one's and two's—but it is as different as day and night from the way I've seen it come before. If the Lord can do it with me, with all I know is wrong with Schaeffer, with one's and two's, He can do it with hundreds too if He wishes. . . . On this last trip at one place . . . even though [I spoke] through translation, I saw them weep as I presented the wonders of our Lord. I am sure the Lord did it and not I. And whether it is one or a crowd, when that comes I am at rest.

. . . I know I've made mistakes and I know I've sinned. And where I know it, I have tried to make it right with those I have hurt, to confess it to the Lord and try to follow His way. . . . My inclination is to think that Christ meant it in a very literal way when He said to seek the lower seats. That does not mean, as I see it, that we should refuse the higher if the Lord takes us there, but He should do the taking. I regret the times in my life when this has not been the case. . . .

I am not sure as to what my future is. . . . I am not at all sure whether or not the rest of my life is meant for Europe. A new trouble has just arisen here because of the work we are doing in Champéry, and it could mean that our police permit will be lost. I guess that this will happen at least some day in this Roman Catholic canton. . . . I came to Europe because I thought I had the Lord's leading in it, and I will leave if I feel I have the same. . . .

[Through the recent difficulties I have faced], the Lord taught me more than I ever knew of the greatness of the Lord and the smallness of any man—and the corresponding importance of pleasing the Lord, and the lack of importance of pleasing any particular man. . . . [In spite of all that has happened there is no question of] personal discouragement, for I am probably less discouraged than I have ever been since those bright days when I first saw the face of the Lord, and before my feet got stuck in the problems of the prestige of man. . . .

. . . Because of our past closeness [I have written these] seventeen pages of handwriting to you. The longest letter I have written—I think—since I was courting Edith! . . .

Love from Edith to Hope, and from all of us to all of you our warmest greetings. I pray for you often and thank God for you.

In our Lord,
Francis A. Schaeffer

[The following note was added at the end of the letter:]

"Oh this self-love, this self-will! It is the Devil of Devils! Lord Jesus, may Thy blessed Spirit purge it out of all our hearts!"

Whitefield

From the Ends of the Earth

[The Schaeffers remained in Switzerland during 1952 and early 1953, returning to the U.S. in April of 1953. They continued in their work for Children for Christ and to a lesser extent for the International Council of Christian Churches. But it was their personal ministry among individual students, and to others who came to the Chapel in Champéry, where the Schaeffers saw the real moving of the Spirit. The following excerpt, written to a foreign missionary in the Persian Gulf, gives a glimpse into their emerging ministry which foreshadows the work of L'Abri.]

2nd February, 1953   Chalet Bijou
                             Champéry, Switzerland

Dear Dr. Larson,

Thank you so much for your letter of January 8. . .

How we rejoice in your word that this has been your

happiest Christmas in Arabia, and how we thank God for this one who has found Christ as His Savior. We often think of you there—and I remember the story you once told of your own encouragement when one night rain came and in the morning the desert was green with seeds that had been hidden away and waiting only the falling of the rain. I am sure that God in His own time will water and bring forth the increase for your many years of faithfulness there in that land of hard hearts.

On our part this has been our best winter season too, with a chance to give a testimony to people from many countries. We have had some very fine and clear professions of faith. It is amazing how the Holy Spirit works in bringing people from the ends of the earth down to this little mountain chalet. I feel as though Chalet Bijou is really a spiritual maternity hospital, as on our knees we thank God for those souls who have been born into His family here. I really have never seen anything like it. With so many people coming down our little path, it makes a severe problem when sometime soon we have to think about packing to return to the States. On the other hand, of course, talking about the things of the Lord always comes first, and when someone comes who wants to know about the Lord, all other things must wait.

The "problem" [which I mentioned in such a sketchy way in my last letter] is not hardship. Edith and I do not consider we have any. I think it is true that a good many Americans would not be happy here with our cold house and semi-isolation, and . . . I guess a good many would not feel that the environment intellectually made them feel at home. But for Edith and myself none of these things are true. . . . When we consider the hardships of some of the rest of you, any we might have is nothing.

Thus, this is not the problem at all. The problem is simply . . . the mistakes that have been made [in our movement]. . . . However, I do not want to write to anyone about it, though I would be happy to have you talk of it with our Father on your knees before Him. . . .

I do not want you to think we are discouraged. We are not; it is rather the opposite. We have found such personal joy in observing the Holy Spirit in the various aspects of our work here that we just wish everyone could share it with us. . . .

May the Lord bless you, and do pray for us.

Cordially yours in Christ,
Francis A. Schaeffer

Organizational Machinery or the Holy Spirit

[After returning in April of 1953, the Schaeffers stayed in the U.S. until September of 1954. During this time Dr. Schaeffer taught Pastoral Theology at Faith Theological Seminary. But more important, Schaeffer spoke 346 times during the 515 days they were in the States on the recurrent theme of "the deeper spiritual life." His letters during this period are replete with this theme, as may be seen in this excerpt written from the U.S. to a Christian friend in Lausanne, Switzerland.]

April 3, 1954   6117 Lensen Street
                                 Phila., Penna.

Dear Mrs. Reeves:

Thank you so much for the letter which you wrote to me. Please convey my warmest greetings to your husband and to all your family. . . .

You will be interested to know that in some ways this time back here [during the last few months] has been a high point in my ministry. I have had several series of meetings on the deeper spiritual life—not for those who are not Christians, but for those who are Christians, calling them and myself at the same time to a deeper walk with our dear Lord. It has been a real blessing. For the first time in my ministry I have seen on the part of some of God's dear children a real crying after an increased holiness in their walk. Surely this is the thing we need above all else—that we who are born-again Christians may be more completely committed to our dear and our lovely Lord. . . .

Our plans have now been definitely made and, the Lord willing, we are sailing from New York on September 1st to return to our home in Champéry and probably five more years of the work there. . . .

Yes, in some ways I think you are right concerning the experience of Goforth. I think it is most important to call the Lord's people to a deeper spiritual walk and to go on as the Lord leads us. On the other hand, I don't think [that the deeper spiritual walk is] in antithesis to an organization. And yet, I must say that it does seem to me that so often organization becomes a means to an end in itself. So often it takes so much energy to turn over all the machinery that the work never gets finished. And so often we put the machinery in the place of the Holy Spirit, feeling that if we can just get organized enough then the thing is sure to go on and be successful.

Of course, this is all very wrong, and not only wrong but wicked. We must realize that it is only the Holy Spirit who can give the power, and we must realize that the only motivation which pleases our dear Lord is our love for Him. Merely keeping machinery turning, and getting all mixed up in the self-aggrandizement that so often goes with a large organization, completely casts aside this primary motive of love to the Lord and a dependence then on the one source of true Christian power—the Holy Spirit.

Thus I increasingly see the dangers involved in organization, and I do think that most of us get the cart before the horse. That is, we organize first and then go forward, rather than growing close to one another through spiritual and personal contacts and then letting whatever organization grow naturally out of that—as the tree puts forth the leaf and then the bud and then the flower as the Lord leads.

These things are becoming a problem to me increasingly as an individual. I see the need for Christians across the face of the earth who are indeed brothers in Christ, standing on the fundamentals of the faith and separated from unbelief, to come into personal fellowship one with the other to the praise of our Lord. And yet how quickly such a thing can grow into that which is merely cold, formal, and dead. The cry of my heart is that God may have mercy on us.

Surely if there has ever been a dark age in history, and one which needs a calling forth unto a deeper spiritual walk and a close waiting upon our dear God, this is our generation. The longer I am back in the United States, the more I tremble for my beloved land. I wonder if we are not coming close to the end of the civilization. How much sin there is, how much darkness, how much that makes one heartsick. There is always sin in the world, but it seems to be growing dark indeed, and surely this should be a call to us to a closer walk to our dear Lord than we have ever had.

We all do send our greetings to all of you and would be happy to keep in touch with you. Thank you so much for the photograph which you sent. Please greet your father and mother for me as well.

Cordially yours in Christ,
Francis A. Schaeffer

The Pain of Death or the Pain of Birth

[Written shortly after the Schaeffers arrived back in Champéry, Switzerland. The person to whom the letter was written is not known, though evidently he or she was close to the Schaeffers, as is suggested by the last paragraph and the tone of the letter as a whole.]

October 11, 1954   Chalet Bijou
                          Champéry, Switzerland

Dear Friend:

Thank you for your note of September 20. It encouraged my heart. How lovely is the Lord, and how wonderfully He is always waiting for us to come to Him and know His peace and joy.

Yes, the time has been difficult, and yet the peace we have known through it makes it exceedingly precious. Since writing to you from the boat, our son, two years of age, has had polio. He began it on the boat, but we did not know what it was. His left leg is affected, but the doctor now gives us good hope that he may return to normal.

Events since we have seen each other make me more sure than ever that the Lord is calling some of us indeed to learn all that the blood of Christ and the indwelling Holy Spirit should mean to us in this present life. Increasingly, I believe that the Devil fears this above all else. Doctrinal rightness and rightness of ecclesiastical position are important, but only as a starting-point to go on into a living relationship—and not as ends in themselves.

When you looked over my article in London for the *Reformation Review* I remember you said, "They will not like this." I replied that I knew, but I did not realize how deep a wound I touched. I find I am being pursued into my work here, and that a determined and successful effort was made in Philadelphia to turn some of the Europeans away from these spiritual matters, and to make them fasten their eyes on loyalty to the external machinery and human leadership. I am sorry. The personal may rest, but I grieve for the work of God. Yet the Lord has given me many wonderful encouragements also; and I do feel that He is calling many of His own into the place of deeper communion.

Would there ever be a time when you could come to Switzerland to meet with others of like mind—to fellowship in

the quietness of the Alps with a small number as we did together that night in your home? We would like to entertain you in
our home. I believe that the pain you have felt, and I have felt,
is not the pain of death, but the pain of birth in a day of
blessing, as the whole body is made more ready for the Bridegroom's coming. Surely the birth pains mean little if such a
result is born through our dear Lord's grace.

With warm greetings in the
slain and risen Lamb,
Francis A. Schaeffer

The Innermost Circle Is the Spiritual

[Since returning to Switzerland in September of 1954, Dr.
Schaeffer was receiving considerable criticism from within the
Bible Presbyterian denomination and from "the movement" as
a whole over his call for a deeper spiritual walk and the need
for truly spiritual devotional literature. Schaeffer was accused
of presenting "slanted" views and "impractical" ideas which
were thought to be implicitly critical of the movement. The
following is Schaeffer's response to one of his critics concerning an article on the need for devotional literature. Copies of
the letter were sent to two other men who also were critical of
Schaeffer's views on this.]

November 12, 1954   Chalet Bijou
                           Champéry, Switzerland
Dear Ted,
Your letter of November 8 arrived yesterday. Thank you
for it. . . .
First I want to thank you for your observations about the
article concerning its vagueness. I read it over again and somewhat agreed. Hence I added another ending and made a few
small changes in the article itself, which I think largely takes
care of this part of it.

But on the fact that you feel it is "sufficiently slanted to be loaded," I do not agree. (I guess if this letter is to be worth writing I had better say freely what I think, for I am writing in the hope that it will be helpful.) . . .

[With a very few exceptions, our movement has] produced practically no devotional literature nor serious study toward a devotional frame of mind. I include myself in this very strongly. Thinking back through the years over my own preaching, writing, and thinking, I am ashamed at this point. . . . God willing, Edith and I want to go on in these matters in which we feel we are only babes. . . .

As I see it, all devotional thinking and material largely falls under four heads:

1. *A call to God's people to the spiritual and to the supernatural.* That is, to live on the plane of a wisdom higher than, and often contrary to, the wisdom of the world; to live in the power of the Holy Spirit in the small as well as large things; to practice doing what the world would consider stupid, in faith that it will please the Lord because it is right.

2. *A call to show forth the love we should show toward God, our brothers, and all mankind*—whether saved or lost, friends or enemies. And a call to stop the hypocrisy of raising the banner of love and then forgetting it. (Let me say at once, and again very strongly, that in my preaching and in my writing in this regard, these matters speak first of all to my own heart.) However, to be worthwhile, this must be practical. For example, in the case of the separatist movement we must honestly face the question of the proper relationship between God's command for the purity of the visible church, and His equal command for an exhibition of the unity of the whole body of Christ.

3. *A call to an absolute loyalty to the headship of Christ and to the leadership of the Holy Spirit.* This cannot help but bring with it the recognition that loyalty to human leadership tends to replace this in a sinful way—i.e., loyalty to organiza-

tions and movements have always tended over time to take the place of loyalty to the person of Christ.

4. *A call to remember that the Church has one duty primarily—namely, the preaching of the gospel*—and that it should not get sidetracked into putting second things first. This cannot help but bring with it the recognition that the primary agencies (above all the church, but also home and foreign mission boards) always tend to be reduced to being merely a means to an end in favor of other types of agencies and organizations. . . .

Through these past four years I have wrestled with this in a way that would sound dramatic if I would try to put it into words, and I have come to my conclusions. The only way that I dare to walk before God [is in accord with His leading in these matters]. I do not judge anyone else in this. I only know the message the Lord has put on my own heart, and which I must speak regardless of the cost. It has already cost me something, and may cost more. . . .

I believe most strongly . . . that our efforts in Christian service fall into three concentric circles: the outer circle is *the apologetic* and defensive. (This is an important portion of Christian activity and should never be minimized, but it is not the heart. . . .) The middle circle is inside the outer one and is more central. This is *the intellectual* statement of the doctrines of the Christian faith in a positive way. (This to me is an even more important portion of Christian activity, but if it stands alone, it still is not Christianity.)

The innermost circle is *the spiritual*—the personal relationship of the individual soul with a personal God, including all that is meant in the apostolic benediction when we say, "The communion of the Holy Spirit be with you all." It is this last, innermost circle with which the devotional deals and without which Christianity is not really Bible-believing.

To me there is no alternative but to ask for God's grace to

keep these three circles in proper position in my own life—to meditate upon this and wrestle with its complete meaning and practice in my own life as I have not wrestled with anything since I wrestled as an agnostic with the claims of Christ as Savior. . . .

I would ask the three of you to be praying for us. A number of things have occurred even since leaving the States which make us feel we face certain decisions. We long to know the Lord's will, and as far as we know our own hearts we long to do His will. By His grace, may you all, and we, forever love Him more and know Him better on a personal level.

With warmest personal regards,

In the slain and risen Lamb,
Francis A. Schaeffer

Living in the Supernatural Now

[To a Finnish Christian leader and coworker with the Schaeffers who had expressed interest in associating with the International Council of Christian Churches. Written just two days before the Schaeffers received notification from the Swiss authorities that they must leave Switzerland within six weeks for "having had a religious influence in the village of Champéry." The book mentioned in the fifth paragraph is the first draft of *True Spirituality*, which was not published until sixteen years later, after a number of Dr. Schaeffer's other books had already been published.]

February 12, 1955   Chalet Bijou
                                     Champéry, Switzerland

Dear Hlinka:

Thank you so much for your Christmas greetings—especially the lovely picture of you and all of your family. Thank you too for your letter of December 21st.

I hope you will excuse my not writing to you at an earlier date, but really this has been a most difficult time. However, the Lord has been wonderfully good in it all, and we would not have missed the difficult times as He has seemed increasingly close to us through them. . . .

Our permit to live here in the Roman Catholic portion of Switzerland has not yet arrived. We are resting that with the Lord, and we are not sure what the future will hold for us in this. Switzerland is divided into Protestant and Roman Catholic cantons, and the Roman Catholic section is about as closed as Italy.

With all this we have had many encouragements in the work, and the Lord has led us to form a small International Church, made up largely of those who have been saved here in our home, from various parts of the world. So far it is indeed small, with only thirteen members. But I think the Lord may have a real future for it. So far the members are made up of two Swiss, one Czechoslovakian who is living in Switzerland, one girl from Argentina who now lives in Hamburg, two in England, and three in the United States—plus Mrs. Schaeffer and the three girls.

It would be a great joy to us if the Lord does lead in our coming to Finland next autumn. We will pray that the Lord will lead you and us clearly in this, but I do hope it works out. Increasingly I feel a burden to see those of us who are Christians go deeper in the Christian life. If the Lord opens the way for us to come to Finland, the desire of my heart would be to give messages on the deeper spiritual life. Insofar as our permit has not yet come, we have not been able to travel in these last months, and a portion of the time I have been working on a book. The Lord willing, its title will be *Living in the Supernatural Now.* This, I think, would be a good general topic for the series I would hope to give there in Finland. . . .

It has occurred to me that I have a responsibility in a

personal capacity to you as a friend [to confide in you concerning a series of critical problems within the structures of the separatist movement. These problems may be summarized as follows]: *First,* I believe there is very little waiting upon God, and very little done that could not be done through super-salesmanship, super-money-raising, and super-politicking. *Second,* it seems to me there is very little of the love of God exhibited, [especially in the] expression of that love toward our brothers in Christ with whom we differ. *Third,* there has been a tremendous demand for loyalty to human leadership. . . . This frightens me as to the future. On my part, I feel increasingly in the other direction—that if we are to know the fullest blessing of God, there must be no final loyalty to human leadership of organizations, or even to organizations as such. Rather, we must urge each other not even to give final authority to principles *about* Christ, but only to the *person* of Christ. *Fourth,* it seems to me that the purpose of the church—to preach the gospel—has been forgotten. With this has come a great "political" emphasis which disturbs me greatly.

I do not know where all this leaves Edith and myself [in our association with these men and organizations]. I have not changed my mind in the need for purity in the visible church. And yet I see that a combat for the faith must flow from an ever closer walk with God and not take the place of it. I do feel that there is a growing number of the Lord's children who feel a deep need for spiritual reality. It can only be my prayer that somehow the Holy Spirit will move to bring forth an abundance of life. May God grant mercy to us. And if it can be in His will, may we yet see the church make herself ready for the Bridegroom in a way we have not yet seen.

May the Lord bless you and us, and lead us ever closer to Him. Edith sends her warmest greetings to you and your wife along with my own.

Cordially yours in the dear Lord,
Francis A. Schaeffer

I Have Stayed on the Train a Long While

[Written to a personal friend (though his name was not used in the salutation) shortly after the Schaeffers' lives had been turned upside down by the events over the last year. Their son Franky, now two, had contracted polio while on the boat returning to Switzerland in September of 1954. Early in 1955 Susan had her first attack of rheumatic fever. In February their chalet was narrowly missed by an avalanche, and then on the same day (February 14) they received notice from the police that they must leave Switzerland, permanently, by March 31. There followed then a truly miraculous series of events whereby the Schaeffers were able to obtain a permanent residency permit and purchase Chalet les Mélèzes in the village of Huémoz. Edith Schaeffer writes that "without our realizing it, L'Abri had started with our first meal in Chalet les Mélèzes" on April 1, 1955 *(L'Abri,* p. 123).

[From this point on, the Schaeffers decided that they would (as Mrs. Schaeffer writes) "ask God that our work, and our lives, be a demonstration that He does exist; not just for six weeks, not for three months, but for as long as He would continue to lead us to live in this manner" (*L'Abri,* p. 124). On June 4, 1955, the Schaeffers decided to resign as missionaries supported by the Independent Board for Presbyterian Foreign Missions. They had no other commitment for support, nor any other sources of regular income. They had no plan for the future, praying instead for the direct leading of God in everything they did. At this point Priscilla was eighteen and attended the University of Lausanne, Susan was fourteen, Debbie was ten, and Franky was almost three. It is remarkable that this turning-point and total redirection of the Schaeffers' life came when the Schaeffers were already in their forties. Dr. Schaeffer's letter here was written one month after their resignation and comes in response to one of a number of inquiries concerning their decision to resign and their plans for the future.]

July 11, 1955   Chalet les Mélèzes
                               Huémoz sur Ollon, Switzerland

Dear Friend in Christ:

Thank you for your letter.

It is difficult to write to you, for if one is going to say anything, one must almost say much, and this I do not wish to do, for I believe that I have prayerfully discharged what has been my duty before the Lord. And now I rest it in His hands. I am writing approximately the same letter to two of you whom I love in the Lord and who have written to me.

I will only say that if I had had no problems in my mind concerning "the movement" thirteen months ago, that which has occurred in the last one year . . . has been enough to have brought me to the conclusions to which I have come.

I can only say to you that I do love you in the Lord. I am sure that you do not at this moment feel the need of my sorrow for you, but I am sorrowful for you. For I have watched men dear to my heart disturbed under injustices to others, insinuations, and half-truths, who have then become accustomed to excusing these matters for the "good of the cause" or the "good of the movement"—until the men whom I have known in the past seem to have died.

Or they have at some point spoken up and been "liquidated."

I have stayed on the train a long while, until its speed has become quite high. My stepping off has been painful, and I am well aware that the bruising I have had thus far (especially through unfounded insinuations) is not the end of the price to be paid for having spoken my mind before the Lord. But no price is too high to pay to have a free conscience before God. The problem is not one of loyalty or lack of loyalty to a "cause" or "movement"; it is the problem of loyalty to the person of Christ.

May the Lord lead you and lead us that we may not deny His existence through lack of faith, nor deny His character in either His holiness or His love. My personal affection continues for you, and we trust that one day you will again visit our home. We would ask you to pray for us. Our greetings to Mrs. Lennert, whom we hope is feeling altogether well.

Yours in the lovely Lord,

Francis A. Schaeffer

Counterfeit Spiritual Reality

[Miss Smith, who had corresponded extensively with Dr. Schaeffer in the past, was involved with the Independent Board for Presbyterian Foreign Missions. Her letter to the Schaeffers would have been written shortly after she heard about the Schaeffers' resignation from the Mission. Schaeffer's long response reveals many of the fundamental principles that determined his thinking, and the whole direction of his life from this point on. Most of the letter is included here.]

August 8, 1955   Chalet les Mélèzes

Huémoz sur Ollon, Switzerland

Dear Miss Smith:

Thank you so much for your letter of July 24. As you said that you were staying in Maine through the month of August, we are sending this to you there and trust that it will reach you safely.

It would be impossible for Edith and myself to tell you what an encouragement your letter was to us. The Lord has been so very gentle in giving us the encouragement which He knows we need, at just the movement we have needed it, through all this time. And your letter was one of those occasions, for we had just recently received Dr. Nystrom's "Statement."

I wish we could have a time to talk and pray together, but we do want you to know that we have felt very much and increasingly that it is a deep spiritual principle that Christians should not vindicate themselves. It has seemed to us that the feverish sending out of long mimeograph letters, which has become so much a part of the "separated movement," is the antithesis of this principle when one's own person is involved. Thus, through this past thirteen months we have asked God to exhibit through us the same mind that He exhibited when "He answered not again." This has been most difficult at times, as you well know, especially when "half-truths," which were really deceptions of a serious sort, were used against not only our work and judgment, but also our character. On the other hand, it is quite clear that the flesh can always find an excuse for answering in any particular instance. Therefore, when these men placed themselves in a completely untenable position at certain points through all of this, and when the truthfulness of their statements could have easily been shown to be lacking, Edith and I have only spread these things before the Lord and asked Him to do with them what He would.

For the last several weeks I have prayed especially that if the Lord would have an answer given beyond what we have felt led to give, that He in His gentleness would lay this upon the heart of one of His dear children of His choosing . . . without any activity to that end on our part. Saturday we received a copy of your letter to Dr. Nystrom [sent to us by Dr. Marshall, in which you came to our total defense]. We can only say that we bowed our heads and worshiped the Lord.

I do not even feel free to say thank you to you, for I well understand that what you wrote you did not write . . . for our sakes. . . . To Edith and myself it is a miracle that you were led to write your letter so clearly and touching the depths of the whole matter. . . . This once more shows God's hand in our own leading, just as completely as did the arrival of the thousand dollars for the house or any of those other remarkable and gentle kindnesses of the Lord which He has used to show us that we have correctly understood His voice.

Miss Smith, we are increasingly convinced that the real

problem in the "separated movement" is a spiritual one. I am convinced after much thought and prayer that we are observing a tragedy the magnitude of which we who are so close to it cannot yet adequately judge. I will tell you the depth of my own conclusion, though as you can understand I would not want it to have wide publication. I believe that the tragedy is somewhere in the following direction. It seems to me that just prior to 1900 we can see an exhibition of New Testament Christianity which was as close to the primitive church as can be found at any time since the days of the New Testament—nearer to the primitive church than even the days of the Reformation. I am thinking of something that was not an organization, not even a "movement," but a clear moving of the Holy Spirit in a number of His dear children. I am thinking of the Welsh revival, the early English Keswick men, Mrs. Penn Lewis, Amy Carmichael, G. Campbell Morgan, F. B. Meyer, Andrew Murray, Miss Seltau in London, the China Inland Mission, etc. It seems to me, in having read with care a great deal of the material flowing from these people, that they did understand the spiritual reality of the Lord's work done in the Lord's way, and a commitment in practical ways to the headship of Christ and the leadership of the indwelling Holy Spirit.

With this came a deep understanding that the battle is not against flesh and blood, and that real participation in this battle has to be through the practical moment by moment leading of the Holy Spirit and with spiritual weapons. Thus, the spiritual became the central, the important thing. External results were seen to be only valid insofar as they flowed from the reality of this central communion with God. This does not mean that I would agree with all they wrote, but there is no question in my mind that they did understand New Testament Christianity at its heart.

It seems to me that three external and observable results flowed from this proper internal spiritual reality. First, there flowed an outreach in evangelism which clearly was not a result of human talent and energy. Second, a certain external exhibition was presented. I am thinking for example of the C.I.M.'s miraculous expansion without the appeal for funds, and certainly Biblically correct matters of healing in bodily health, etc. Third, as one reads the writings of this circle of His children, one finds a remarkably clear combat arising against liberal Protestantism. This combat had great strength—as for example when the China Inland Mission determined to continue its completely Biblical character in the early days of Dr. Hoste's directorship; and in the loving and yet effective questions raised concerning the weaknesses of the World Missionary Conference of 1910.

Even at the time of the Welsh revival, however, those involved recognized that Satan was disrupting the full realization of fruit by producing counterfeit expressions of external signs (point two above) as found in the rising flood of Pentecostalism. It is quite clear that Satan used this counterfeit to rob Wales of all that would have been expected from the Welsh revival.

It seems to me that we who are living fifty years after this period have seen the rise of counterfeits in not just one of the points above, but in all three. And it has been my sober conclusion that the counterfeit to number three has been ourselves. . . . I have realized before the face of the Lord that . . . the so-called "separated movement" is a part of this. This does not mean that I question the salvation of the individuals who are involved in these counterfeits. But I do believe that the only solution is to get back to the spiritual correctness of those who lived fifty years ago in the circle I mentioned above. . . . Perhaps the greatest tragedy in this whole matter is that . . . the Christians of our generation have tended to be repulsed from the Scriptural position of the purity of the visible church because of this counterfeit.

But who can blame the Christian world from being repulsed, rather than drawn to . . . purity in the church when they observed what has occurred in the orbit of those who claim to represent this Scriptural principle. . . . Those who have any sensitivity to New Testament Christianity are naturally going to be completely repulsed by the failure to show forth God's love in any way, and by the devouring criticism leveled against those who would speak for a balance in showing forth the love of God and the holiness of God.

Edith thinks I should add one more thought so that there will be no possibility of misunderstanding. This is as follows: as "Pentecostalism" stresses the *external signs* without the internal realities, so also the "separated movement" stresses certain *external and minute forms of separation* from organizational unbelief without resting this on the supernatural, internal spiritual realities. And because of this, the separated movement excuses all sorts of other things which strike down both the exhibition of the love of God and His holiness.

One would faint if it were not for the knowledge that the Lord can do what He will. . . . If even a few in Christendom get back to the spiritual foundation, the Lord can move upon the bride of Christ through the Holy Spirit—so that she might show forth the fact that God does truly exist, and that both the love and the holiness of God can be exhibited in the power of the Holy Spirit.

I need not tell you that Edith and I feel much the need of prayer.

On the other hand, surely no one has ever been treated more gently by the Lord. The marvels continue: both in hearts opened by the Holy Spirit, in a way we have never seen before among these university young people, and in the meeting of our financial needs. He is wonderful, and that surely is enough. . . .

Edith sends her love to you with my own. She hasn't been feeling well the last couple of days, and as a matter of fact is typing this for me in bed; thus please excuse the mistakes.

With affectionate greetings,

> In the Lamb slain for us,
> Francis A. Schaeffer

Stones in the Midst of Jordan

[To a close friend and supporter of the Schaeffers, in response
to his letter of encouragement, which also included information concerning the reaction to the Schaeffers' resignation.]

August 27, 1955   Chalet les Mélèzes
                            Huémoz sur Ollon, Switzerland
Dear Garrett,
        Thank you so much for your letter. It is always so good to
hear from you. And thank you for the five dollars enclosed for
L'Abri Fellowship. We would ask you to keep praying. So far it
has seemed to us that the Lord has made it clear that we have
not missed His voice. [This is clear] both in the way individuals
seem to be led here in a miraculous manner, with hearts prepared by the Holy Spirit, and in the way He has supplied our
material needs, also in a manner that seems wonderful to us.
        Thank you too for the balloon for Franky. Balloons are
always such a joy to both of our younger children. . . .
        The Lord has led Edith and myself along so very gently in
all this. We are often upon our knees thanking Him for His
gentleness; for in our case He has so quietly led us along, and
each step of the way He has given us something better before
He took away the lesser. The last year and three months have
been the hardest of our lives with dart hurled after dart. But the
stones He has given us from the midst of Jordan have been
overwhelmingly wonderful. It is our prayer for you and your
wife that you may at every turn of the way know His protecting
arm.
        Incidentally you should know that when Edith and I
stepped out of the Independent Board we really did not have
any promise of support—nor had we asked for any. He has
cared for us for these first two months in a way that over-
whelms us. We would not presume to tell you what we even
might imagine you should do; each one of us must stand direct-

ly before the Lord's face. But we would bear our testimony that although the decisions we have made on principle have cost us everything into which we had put twenty years of interest and work, still he has given us a quietness of heart. And in these hearts which He has prepared and sent to us, we have seen the Holy Spirit working in a new way. And we have lacked neither bread nor friends.

May the Lord bless you. I pray for you and ask that you pray for me.

With warm personal greetings from Edith and myself to your wife and children as well as to you, and with love from the girls and little Frank,

Your friend,
Francis A. Schaeffer

How Much We Have to Unlearn by His Grace

[The next two letters are to a minister friend in the Bible Presbyterian denomination. Although the letters between Schaeffer and Gordon discuss various aspects of the controversy and conflict in the denomination, by this time the tone is more that of outside observers who are saddened by what they see rather than participants caught up in the conflict. The portions selected here from these letters give early glimpses into the life of L'Abri as well as something of the Schaeffers' daily dependence on the Lord and their daily spiritual walk.]

January 9, 1956   Chalet les Mélèzes
                         Huémoz sur Ollon, Switzerland

Dear Gordon:

It is with real embarrassment that I say I am sorry that it has been so long since I wrote to you. I see that your letter was written September 28! That does not seem possible, although the knowledge that I owed you a letter has been nagging at me for a long time. I trust that you will forgive me, for it is not that

I have failed to think of you and pray for you, but we have been running about 250 letters behind. . . . I cannot tell you how much I appreciated your long letter. We thank the Lord for the safe arrival of David, and trust that both he and Jennifer continue to do well.

We have been overflowingly busy—overflowingly because the business has been a matter of the fullness of the Lord's blessing on the work—for which we praise Him. . . .

The Lord in a miraculous way (and I do not use the word "miracle" lightly) opened up the way for us to have holiday services in Champéry. What a victory it was, by the might and the power and the victory of God, over the enemy of souls. We had 175 present on New Year's Eve, and also well attended services on the first and eighth [of January].

The work among the students in Lausanne is also going well, with fifteen or sixteen present each week, meeting in the back room of a cafe near the university. They represent about six nations. We are praying that the Holy Spirit will do exceedingly more around these cafe tables than could be imagined—especially as we remember what the Devil did on the "left bank" of Paris with Sartre, around the cafe tables along *St. Germaine de Pres.* Do pray with us.

We are also having a constant string of G.I.s from Germany. It is indeed overflowing with guests almost always in our home now. The Lord has also wonderfully sent in the needed funds. This to our eyes is a never ending marvel. . . .

. . . The fact that the funds have come in as they have—looking only to the Lord and not asking for funds, not returning to the States to organize anything, and not advertising our needs (except for what Edith writes in her family letters)—all of this has made the reality of our dear Lord greater as the days have gone on. It does not make us feel that the other way is wrong, but for ourselves we are convinced that this is His way for us, and for us a better way. In my devotional reading today I came across this from Amy Carmichael: "Why not ask God to make those who love Him want to help the little children whom He loves, instead of asking help from those who perhaps don't love Him." For ourselves, we are sure He has led us in this direction.

We have gone along from day to day not trying to make plans too definitely, but rather hoping indeed that His plans would be our only plan. The way has been sweet and our hearts have been glad, except as we view our own coldness of heart and habit of returning to the old ways. Indeed we have much to unlearn by His grace. . . .

May the Lord lead you gently. And do pray that He may take much time with us, for we need much time to learn.

Edith sends her love to Jennifer and yourself; we wish we could see your faces.

As ever, your friend,
Francis A. Schaeffer

We Really Have No Plans

February 8, 1956   Chalet les Mélèzes

                                  Huémoz sur Ollon, Switzerland

Dear Gordon:

Thank you again for your letter of January 13. We did appreciate so much your writing so quickly and so fully. . . . Your letters really are a joy. I mean that with all my heart. I do feel, in the providence of God, that among those who write me, you and I see things most nearly alike. I trust that is because it is His mind. . . .

. . . The [spiritual] battle is often terrific. But the Lord does continue to lead us along. We need your prayers constantly, more than you can know. But I do believe that He is giving a demonstration here of His existence. I believe more and more that *this* is truly the central task of the Christian—to give the

Lord the opportunity to exhibit His existence. To the extent to which this is true here, we are thankful. . . .

Really, we have no plans for the future. For the first time in my life, I think, I have no plans. I am not sure how this place and our work is going to develop. But Edith and I are constantly amazed how He sends people with spiritual needs here from literally everywhere—and the way He is sending in the funds to care for them. . . . We have found what Amy Carmichael found long ago: that the decisions of a growing work demand that the One who directs be constantly at hand.

May the Lord lead Jennifer and you, and may He lead us. We send our love to you,

As ever, in the lovely Lamb,
Francis A. Schaeffer

Betraying the One We Love

[This remarkable letter shows Dr. Schaeffer's desire to set right mistaken judgments which he had made many years ago. It also mentions that Schaeffer destroyed many of his old letters in 1955. Though he does not say what letters were destroyed and why, it seems likely that these would have concerned the controversies and conflicts in which he had been embroiled. This is suggested by the fact that these letters were destroyed in 1955 when the Schaeffers made their decisive break with the past. It would seem that this was part of Dr. Schaeffer's efforts to put the past behind him and set right whatever he could.]

August 29, 1956   Chalet les Mélèzes
                               Huémoz sur Ollon, Switzerland

Dear Mr. Lohmann:

Perhaps you will not remember me, but I was in your home in 1947. At that time you gave me certain addresses in Germany, as I was going to Europe for three months, making the initial European contacts and looking forward to the formation of an international council of churches.

Later, in June 1948, I wrote to you just before I sailed to Europe for the formation of the International Council of Christian Churches in Amsterdam and to remain here in Europe as a missionary under the Independent Board for Presbyterian Foreign Missions. You answered with a four-page letter dated July 6, 1948. I remember that I answered you, but I do not have a copy of my answer in my files.

About a year ago I was going through some old letters, destroying many of them, and in those letters I found yours of 1948. Upon reading it over I realized that the central judgments in your letter, which in 1948 I felt were mistaken, I have in the intervening years come to realize were correct.

I did not destroy your letter when I found it in my past correspondence, but put it aside wondering if I should write and tell you that I had come to know that you were right and I was wrong in our exchange of letters. In the past year from time to time I have come upon your letter among my unanswered correspondence where I had placed it. But I have always put it aside for more pressing things. However, last night Mr. and Mrs. Schumacher came to my Bible class here in this area where I now live, and I felt in this that the Lord spoke to me not to put off writing to you any longer.

Through a protracted process of spiritual wrestling with the Lord covering several years, I have come to agree with what you expressed: "These giant world organizations remind me distinctly of the grain of mustard seed in Matthew 13, 'which *man* took and sowed in *his* field.' " The underlinings are yours, but they express what I have come to think of the matter. This gradually resulted in my resigning from some of the things to which I belonged, and as a result my being dropped from others. The process is still continuing, but at this time (1956) I no longer have connections with any of the large organizations which have been known as "the separated movement."

Let me say that I have not changed my mind concerning the danger from Rome or from "liberal" Protestantism. I have more personal reason to know of that danger than ever before. Mrs. Schaeffer and I lived in the Roman Catholic canton of Valais (Switzerland) from 1949 on. Though we did not live there to evangelize, but as a home from which to travel for our work at that time through Europe (beginning children's Bible classes in homes of Christians in various countries in Europe), still the Lord did open doors in Champéry where we lived, and He blessed with fruit.

Among other things, one of the leading men of the village and of the area, who had been a Roman Catholic in name but an atheist in belief and in practice, came to the Lord. For this we were put out of Valais, and an attempt was made by the Roman Catholic Bishop of Valais to have us put out of all of Switzerland because of our "having a religious influence in the village." The Lord wonderfully intervened in that, and we are now living in the canton of Vaud, and we have walked through the door He has opened to us, especially doing work in Lausanne, etc., among the many foreign university students in Switzerland. I also now have a class in Milan, Italy, among those studying music there from many lands. We are carrying this on as L'Abri Fellowship, having resigned from the Independent Board at the end of last June (1955).

The student work in Lausanne and Geneva has brought us into contact with some of the "liberal" English-speaking (British and American) pastors in Lausanne and Geneva. Again I have found the use of uncamouflaged force in their attempt to shut out the preaching of the gospel.

Thus I have new reason not to have changed my mind concerning the danger either from Rome or "liberal" Protestantism. But I have changed my mind as to that which honors the Lord and the reality of the Holy Spirit in meeting these dangers. In the midst of these matters we have looked only to the Lord, realizing that unless the existence and character of the dear Lord are exhibited in such moments, more is lost in "winning" than would be the case in "losing." I might say in passing that the Lord has honored this, and we have been seeing things in the work here which seem to us to be miracles. . . .

I have come to know that you were completely right when you wrote: "I fear that by organizing Christians all over the world we are doing a very similar thing to that which has been done [by others] and there is no authorization or Biblical grounds. I further fear that very little personal love will radiate from these giant 'steamroller' organizations; that rather there will be considerable animosity towards those who do not wish to join."

I also have come to realize that you were right as you wrote of the lack of love as "the driving motive" in the personal attacks made on other Christians. You especially mentioned the personal attacks made in [one of our periodicals] "on leading brothers."

. . . The Lord has been speaking to me during my prayer times in the quietness of the Alps that it is as important to show forth the love of God as to show forth the holiness of God. And that this surely means that personal attacks (whether against "leading brothers," against little-known brethren in the Lord, or against unbelievers) were completely ruinous spiritually to the Christians who employed or who condoned such personal attack. Hence, I wrote an open letter on this matter, objecting to this sort of thing in general and in particular to [the case of a vicious attack upon a pastor who decided to stay in the Presbyterian Church U.S.A.] . . . even though I personally felt at the time and still do today that [he] had made a mistaken judgment in relation to [this]. . . .

From the time of my writing that open letter on, Mrs. Schaeffer and I have gone through many difficult times. But we would not give up these hard moments, for in them we have found Him completely gentle and enough. I am glad that, by His grace, these difficult times did not come before my objecting to [this] matter, but that my objecting led to them. Indeed, how gentle He is.

In short, thank you for your letter in 1948. I now can well understand what you wrote: "This has been on my heart the last two days, and the greater part has been spent in prayer and thought to enable me to write this letter." Such has been my own experience many times through these past three or four years. Your words, "I have used my Bible to hit and to embarrass those who could not see and read the way I did, like Luther and Zwingli. I regret this time of my life. Our own strength, zeal and enthusiasm ends, usually like Peter's sword attack, in betraying the One we love"—this has become my own experience.

With greetings in the Lamb,
Francis A. Schaeffer

Reality, Heresy, Eastern Religion, and Barth

[Dr. Schaeffer's letters from late 1956 through 1958 continue to stress the central importance of spiritual reality and a moment by moment dependence upon the Lord. But along with this, many of the letters contain fresh new insights and application of these principles. Often these are in the form of a brief paragraph embedded in a long letter on another topic. The following selections, ranging from November 1956 through March of 1958 have been excerpted from six letters and grouped together so as to give an overview of how Schaeffer's thinking was developing during this period. No attempt has been made to identify the recipients, though most of these ideas were written first to very close friends. The paragraphs included below contain some surprising insights, sometimes expressed by Dr. Schaeffer for the first time in writing and shedding new light on the development of his thinking. These grew out of Schaeffer's own experience of trying to live a life in total dependence on the Lord, but at the same time in vital interaction with the world and its ideas. Often these insights were the fruit of hours of conversation with university students in the cafes of Lausanne, Geneva, and Zurich; or all-night discussions with a dozen students in the Schaeffers' chalet; or pages and pages of correspondence with a close friend.]

November 1956   Chalet les Mélèzes
through March 1958   Huémoz sur Ollon, Switzerland

I wish I could put into words what I have increasingly felt in the past few years. I believe that when the Bible says that God is a God of truth, it is saying something far deeper than we usually realize. It is saying that God is truth in the sense that He is the God of *reality*—that there is only *one* God and only *one* reality. And if one does not know this God and the reality which flows from understanding Him (including the world as He made it and as it now is through sin), then one has *no* God and lives in a universe that does not really exist and therefore is untrue in the deep sense of not being real. This, I believe, is what has led to such philosophies as existentialism and logical positivism. Further, I believe this "universe of no God" and unreality is the product of the "great lie" of the father of lies—the Devil—and that it all is a perversion.

• • • • •

The winter's work has started with a rush, and I am constantly amazed at the way the Lord directs. . . . We do believe that one calling which the Lord has given to L'Abri is for various young people to come for a year or so—not only to work in a practical way, but to learn the reality of trusting the Lord, not only in financial needs, but in faith laying hold of the promises of the Lord concerning the practical leadership of the Holy Spirit in daily details. I believe more and more that *trust* can be taught by observation. Edith and I have marveled here as we have placed the choosing of workers in the Lord's hands.

We have seen many times how the Lord has sent just the person we needed at just the moment someone else was leaving without previous planning on our part. So far L'Abri has had eleven workers, and it is really amazing the way the whole thing has fit together. . . .

But you should know that this does not mean that we do not often face troubles. . . . This is not the case. Time after time we have come to what has seemed to be close to a dead end, and it is just at that point that we feel the fact of trust stands or falls. Thus at such a time we have special days of prayer, and time after time it has been immediately on the day of prayer itself that the answer has come. This month we have very much gone through such a period. With [two more workers] coming it means a large step forward in financial need. Without going into the details, after prayerful and lengthy consideration we did feel that we have adequate certainty that the Lord was leading in their coming. But there is no promise from human sources of any increase in the finances to meet the needs of their being here. Thus, this month is a month of wrestling in a very special way before the Lord at this point.

• • • • •

[When it comes to] waiting in a practical way for the moving of the Spirit . . . I do feel there has been something wrong with our whole theological system—not just recently, but extending back to old Princeton and the old Dutch schools when they were completely orthodox. It is something difficult to put into words, but there seems to be a certain academic outlook, or perhaps a limiting of the Biblical truths to the speculative realm.

• • • • •

It is my belief that the Reformation itself, with certain notable exceptions, made a basic error . . . [by making a false] division between the intellectual and the Spiritual. (By the word Spiritual with a capital "S" we are referring to nothing less than a commitment to the Holy Spirit.) . . . I think it is the "pendulum psychology" again.

The Roman Catholic Church had come to teach the *wrong* doctrines. And I feel that most of the Reformation then let the pendulum swing and thought if only the *right* doctrines were taught that all would be automatically well. Thus, to a large extent, the Reformation concentrated almost exclusively on the "teaching ministry of the Church." In other words almost all the emphasis was placed on teaching the right doctrines. In this I feel the fatal error had already been made. *It is not for a moment that we can begin to get anywhere until the right doctrines are taught. But the right doctrines mentally assented to are not an end in themselves, but should only be the vestibule to a personal and loving communion with God.* . . .

Personally I believe church history shows that as this basic weakness in Protestantism developed into a completely dead orthodoxy, then liberalism came forth. Thus, the solution is not to intellectually and coldly just shout out the right doctrines and try to shout down the false liberal doctrines. It is to go back to a cure of the basic error. It is to say "yes" to the right doctrines, and, without compromise, "no" to the wrong doctrines of both Romanism and liberalism—and then to commit our lives to the practical moment by moment headship of Christ and communion of the Holy Spirit.

• • • • •

Increasingly I believe that after we are saved we have only one calling, and that is to show forth the existence and the character of God. Since God is love and God is holy, it is our calling to act in such a way as to demonstrate the existence of God—in other words to be and to act in such a way as to show forth His love and His holiness *simultaneously.* Further, I believe that the failure to show forth either of these is equally a perversion. Of course, in one's own strength it is only possible to show forth *either* love *or* holiness. But to show forth the holiness and love of God simultaneously requires much more.

It requires a moment by moment work of the Holy Spirit in a very practical way. It has become my conclusion . . . that there is something doctrinally wrong with that branch of [extreme] fundamentalism. . . . This wing of "fundamentalism" not only failed to show forth the love of God, but actually considered mentioning the love of God in itself to be a heresy. . . . I believe, however, they are a heresy in their own way in reference to the love of God, just as modernism is a heresy in its own way in regard to the holiness of God.

• • • • •

I do praise the Lord that the Holy Spirit has led you into understanding concerning these matters [i.e., the mistakes of the separatist movement], and I feel that insofar as this is the case you should be most thankful to Him for it and realize that you now have a tremendous responsibility of using the understanding He has given you.

I feel that you are in a place of danger, and you must find your strength directly from the Lord. I feel that you are in a place of danger because your tendency would now naturally be to think of the liberal evil as less horrible than it really is. It would seem to me that this would be your danger because, realizing that much of that which is called "fundamental Christianity" also has terrible weaknesses, you would tend to equate the two weaknesses and therefore that of liberalism would tend to seem less of hell than it is.

It is not that I feel less strongly than you concerning the weaknesses of a cold fundamentalism, but liberalism with its denial of the Bible as the Word of God (in either the old Fosdick type of liberalism or the new Barth type of liberalism) destroys all possible authority of an absolute nature. Therefore, I feel liberalism is so completely destructive in the finding of the truth that I would not for a moment even *seem* to equate fundamentalism and liberalism as equal dangers.

• • • • •

One thing I think would interest you in the growth of my own thinking, in the light of contacts with students studying under Barth—but also through contacts with the wide variety of people we have had here, plus my own study over the last few years. I am convinced that most of the young men are taught against too narrow a backdrop, and [are still fighting the old battles of the Reformation]. But in reality this is no longer where we are, either in theory or in practice. Actually the battle is being fought against the backdrop of all the religions of the world which have apostatized from the true religion since the foundation of the world. . . .

To be more specific, it seems to me that most of the evangelicals reviewing Barth, Brunner, etc., misunderstand them because they study them as though they are related only in a certain way to Reformation theology. In reality I believe Barth, Brunner, etc., are understandable only when we have a background of knowledge concerning the problems which Hinduism and Buddhism thought through, and which even Islam thought through. In short, I believe that [modern existential] theology is much more closely related to the perverted truths in the religions of the East than to historic Protestant theology. . . .*

All these contacts here have driven me more and more in the last three years to study Hinduism, Buddhism, and now Islam. I am amazed at what I find—so different from that which is usually given in a "Mission Course." . . .

As I read the half-hearted articles so often given about Barth, Brunner, and so on, it would seem to me . . . that often the conservative critic would be . . . swept off his feet by the subtleties of Barth's thinking . . . when a Hindu would understand Barth much better. I know that my contacts with these people have not been outstandingly successful. But I do think that I see the outlines of something (from this terrific cross section of contacts and from my own study in these areas) that I have never seen before. The marvelous thing is that the Bible has such crystal-clear answers—not only to these intellectual problems, but to the really deep spiritual ones such as personality, the meaning of life, and communion with God. With this I have an increased feeling, not only that the controversy must be carried on rightly, but that we must be sensitive to the battle at hand. The first necessity is to have men who are spiritually sensitive. These men therefore will probably have a natural inclination to shy away from controversy. [They must be men therefore] who are drawn into it because of a sensitivity to the leading of the Holy Spirit and the love of our wonderful Lord. . . .

It is my prayer that the whole church of Christ will be moved. And that from here and there the Lord will raise up men—perhaps from many areas and not just from some of the past lines of division—men committed to the leading of the Spirit and therefore more ready for tomorrow's wider battles.

*At first Schaeffer's suggestion here may seem truly shocking. I believe, however, that he is making an important point which can be successfully defended, and which is even prophetic.

The point is that although existential theologians may use the language of the Reformation, their method and their basic thought forms are fundamentally different from those of the Reformation. Schaeffer asserts that most evangelicals completely misunderstand this because they hear only the "Reformational language" without realizing that it is grounded in radically different thought forms. The influence of Eastern thought forms is especially evident in the theology of some of the more liberal theologians such as Paul Tillich, John Cobb, and Teilhard de Chardin. It may be argued, though, that these thought forms are also present in the less extreme existential theologians. In the late 1960s, there was a growing attempt to synthesize Eastern religion and Christian thought (e.g., the hippie movement, the drug culture, the theology of Alan Watts). This continues today, for example, in the "New Age" movement. Thus Schaeffer showed remarkable insight in recognizing the early influence of Eastern thought forms in Christian theology, and his "shocking suggestion" is in fact borne out in theology and the culture as a whole over the next thirty years.

We Have Seen a Little of the Blazing Glory of God

[The main body of the following letter was written in almost identical form to two of Dr. Schaeffer's closest friends. At this time these are the only two people with whom Schaeffer carried on an extended, personal correspondence. Gordon is identified in connection with the letter included above, dated January 9, 1956. A number of the excerpts in the preceding section were from letters written to Jim, the other recipient of this letter. Jim remained a lifelong close friend of the Schaeffers. He was often the first person with whom Dr. Schaeffer would share a new insight in writing. Jim is a leader in higher education. The letter below shows the profound connection which Schaeffer saw between spirituality, doctrine, and the whole spectrum of reality. It was written while the Schaeffers were on vacation in Spain. The letter is taken mostly from the one written to Gordon, with a few paragraphs inserted for clarification from Jim's.]

October 3, [4], 1958   Alassio
                                    Italy

Dear Gordon [Jim],

Thank you for your letters. You will never know how many times I tried to get started writing to you. The problem is that there are only a couple of people with whom I now carry on a personal correspondence. As I always hope that these letters will be longer, unhappily they tend to be put aside until I will have adequate time for them, and this means they never even seem to get started.

My work over here in contact with so many people often builds a fire in my bones—to get some of the things which I feel are important down on paper. But often both Edith and I seem to be so near to the thin edge of not being able to get on. This, of course, is not conducive to begin trying to write again. . . . Edith and I have been overwhelmed at the way this work has grown since L'Abri was formed a little over three years ago. . . . Thus we wonder what lies ahead, and you will understand why we feel so strongly the need of prayer.

My own feeling and experience, and our experience at L'Abri, has, I do believe, gone deeper and ever deeper in these last years since L'Abri was formed. It seems to me that the real question is what we really believe. It seems to me that we do tend to have two creeds—the one which we believe in our *intellectual assent,* and then the one which we believe to the extent of *acting* upon it in faith. More and more it seems to me that the true level of our orthodoxy is measured by this latter standard rather than the former. And more and more it seems to me that there is no such thing as an abstract Christian dogma—that each Christian dogma can be *experienced* on some level. For example, the Trinity: one might say, how could this be experienced? But in my work with orientals and oriental religions—as well as Western philosophers such as the existentialists—I am convinced that the Trinity is an overwhelming doctrine which gives the world its only possible answer for the reality of personality. Thus, I do believe the Trinity can be *experienced* as the personality of God becomes real to us—as we know His *person* and not just doctrines about Him. And (perhaps most important) this can be experienced when we in some small measure begin to know the reality of His individual leading as we in moment by moment faith truly desire that He, the infinite person, might lead us, the finite persons.

The spiritual steps which meant so much to me just before my furlough [i.e., in 1951-52] and during my furlough [in 1953-54] centered largely around the moment by moment reality of the blood of Christ. I realized then in theory, but now as something deeper than theory, that there is a further step which is more profound in the reality of the universe: this is the reality of taking our place as creatures, willingly and in love, in the presence of the infinite Creator. If we would only stop desiring to be God and, in reality and practice, take our place as creatures, then I think we could get on.

I am not thinking of this in some "mystical" area where God becomes an abstraction, but in the strenuously practical areas of history in which we walk. If we would only allow the Agent of the Trinity, the Holy Spirit, to lead each individual instead of living in the areas of rules which are man-made and quite apart from the absolutes laid down in Scripture. If only we would be willing to have Christ be the true Head, and be willing for the exotic leadership of the Holy Spirit in our individual and corporate lives—rather than stagnifying* the Holy Spirit's leadership of yesterday, as seen in the lives of other men who lived in different historic circumstances, when the infinite eye of God would see today's history as requiring a slightly different or radically different approach; or even stagnifying how the Holy Spirit has led us individually in the past. Why should the Holy Spirit's leading of us today be what it was a year ago, when our historic circumstance is always in a flux? To me these things are not an abstraction. As one small practical application, why do we insist on continuing organizations just because they were useful last week, or last year?

To think of it in our case, how can we dare to say that because the Holy Spirit has led in a certain way for three years this is complete and unchangeable proof that the Holy Spirit will use L'Abri the same way a year from now? Surely this is the walk of faith: not to fall into set phrases or set prayers—but equally not to fall into set patterns which in reality are graves. But, of course, to begin to speak like this, and especially to begin to live like this, will immediately be considered impractical by those who do not understand. But may God grant us the grace to press on, believing that God does exist. He is a *person;* and after we have come under the blood of Christ He will then lead us as His children if we deliberately place ourselves in His hands.

In a practical way we have tried to carry these things out in L'Abri. We are so very aware that it has been mostly poorly done. But Edith and I and some of those with us have been overwhelmed at what the Lord has done on the basis of the poor steps that have been taken. It is not that it does not take more energy. We have found that it does—with the battle and the work taking more from us than merely human plans and human pressing would ever do. But we have seen a little too of

the blazing glory of God at work. Do pray for us, and we do
you. . . .

Edith sends her love along with my own. I do want you to
know how much our correspondence means to me as a help,
and as fellowship with you.

> In the Lamb,
> Francis A. Schaeffer

*"Stagnifying" is a word which Dr. Schaeffer apparently coined with-
out realizing it. By this he seems to mean something which would combine
the meanings of "stagnate" and "magnify." In other words, the meaning
intended here suggests the idea of taking an experience from the past which
may have been valid and good in the context, and then "venerating" this in
the present in an entirely different context—with the result that the experience from the past becomes a stagnant experience in the present.

The Existence and Character of God in This Generation

[To one of the same close friends who received a copy of the
preceding letter.]

March 2, 1959   Chalet les Mélèzes
                            Huémoz sur Ollon, Switzerland

Dear Jim:

Both of us were so glad to get your last letter, though again
the time has stretched on without my answering. . . . We are
constantly amazed at the way the Lord continues to keep our
time so very full in the work, and also how many indications
He does continue to give of His leading and blessing. . . .

Looking back over the past four years, I thought you
would be interested to know a bit of how it looks to us. When
we began, of course, it was easier to make a rather drastic
decision than it otherwise would have been because of all that
had occurred. . . . But even looking back on it after four years

of a very rich time, we still remember that it was not easy with the four children to take that step and begin to put into practice that which had increasingly forced itself upon our mind in the past few years, [namely] of looking only to the Lord in the various areas of work. . . . Since that time we have asked no one except the Lord for funds and . . . every bill has been paid on time. . . . While we vividly remember [this] step of faith . . . [we have clearly seen] the reality of the demonstration that the Lord can care for needs in answer to prayer alone. . . .

We feel the Lord is saying something in this—not that we feel that the Lord would necessarily call anyone else for that which He has called us. But both Edith and I have felt that this work here is not first of all called of the Lord to be an evangelistic one in any sense, but rather to be a demonstration in a small way of [the existence and character of the God who does exist].

As L'Abri will shortly be four years old, we can say that . . . we have had many causes to worship Him [for meeting our needs]. . . . It is not that there have not been numerous times where we have needed to wait in prayer with great care. But we have learned just a little of the fact that if there is no dark place, there is no possibility of trust. . . .

Along with the principle of trusting the Lord . . . we have felt led of the Lord to act upon claiming the blood of Christ in a specific way—to make it possible for us to live together in a very difficult situation that L'Abri puts upon those who live and work here; to live together in love on a level beyond what could be expected by our natural circumstances. Thus, we have tried to keep this principle in practice, before that of mere efficiency in the work. In practice this has meant some long periods of waiting for each other, even though everything in us has made loud noises to get on because some section of the work would suffer (humanly speaking) if we waited. We feel we have much to learn in this area, but it has been a sweet experience to see that this is not idealistic but possible. . . . We are thankful to see that the principles laid down in Scripture do not have to be considered only as principles in the distance.

As time goes on, the Lord has brought so many very unique people here and to the classes. Sitting quietly with them, it has been necessary to place the Word of God face to face with the questions that are hurled without restraint from both Western and Eastern mentalities. More and more it causes me to realize that in reality Christianity is the greatest intellectual system the mind of man has ever touched. It really has been a tremendous experience to sit in classes and in discussions with those who would be considered top flight by the best of the world's standards, and to watch the Word of God literally have an answer for every question across the board. . . . Yet if this is all there is, eventually all it will prove is that Christianity is indeed the best system the mind of man has ever touched. In short, something more is needed in addition if the system is to be proven to be Truth—that which the universe truly is.

And I am convinced that this something in addition must be a demonstration that the existence of God—His character and His acting in history—is not merely theoretical, but a reality in history; not only from 1500 B.C. till 100 A.D., but in *every* generation.

In it all we feel a great need for prayer, for we often feel the battle in a very pressing way. Thus, the knowledge that you are praying for us means so much to all of us here.

In the Lamb,
Francis A. Schaeffer

Finding a Point at Which to Begin

[To a former University of Lausanne student who visited L'Abri frequently while in Lausanne.]

December 20, 1960   Chalet les Mélèzes
                          Huémoz sur Ollon, Switzerland
Dear Linda:

How much your letter of October 30 meant to us. I am so sorry it has been such a long time from the time we received it until I am answering. But you do know the problem here and understand the problem of correspondence. Perhaps I should have handed it over to someone else to answer, and then it would have been answered at an earlier date, but I very much wanted to answer you personally. And with Mrs. Schaeffer's note telling you that I would be writing, I thought it would be all right to wait a little while. And now here it is almost Christmas!

Linda, we all do remember you before the Lord, and especially at our Wednesday night community prayer meetings. You are prayed for regularly as we feel a unity with you in the little International Church, and as one we all love in the Lord. . . .

Linda, the problem of reality in our Christian lives is one which we all must face. It is possible (and here I speak from experience) to be a pastor for years, believing and preaching the Biblical truths—and at the same time, unhappily, to have the reality slide backwards down the hill. The balance is a very fine one, for there is a great deal of weight on the other side of the knife blade. This has always been true, with the emphasis towards mysticism (in a bad sense) being experienced without intellectual comprehension. Falling off on this side of the knife blade certainly is a tragedy and is exhibited in numerous lives in history. Thus the strong doctrinal churches have always leaned against mysticism. Also, in our particular day this is even a greater danger. . . . This is highly complicated because of the relativistic (and subjective) modern theology, and even more complicated because many evangelicals are specifically being influenced by this relativistic and subjective theology.

On the other hand, the danger of orthodoxy, even true orthodoxy, is in falling off the other side of the knife blade: that is, in stating the intellectual position and then placing a period. What we must ask the Lord for is a work of the Spirit . . . to stand on a very thin line: in other words, to state intellectually (as well as understand, though not completely) the intellectual reality of that which God is and what God has revealed in the objectively inspired Bible; and then to live moment by moment in the reality of a restored relationship with the God who is there, and to act in faith upon what we believe in our daily lives.

Now I am sure that this cannot be done in the flesh: it is possible to fall off the knife blade on either side in the flesh. To stand on the knife blade can only be accomplished on the basis of the finished work of the Lord Jesus Christ, through moment by moment faith, in the power of the Spirit.

The practical problem for us individually is to find a point at which we can begin to live moment by moment in reality. Many people in the past have emphasized that the beginning point for them was the reality of victory over sin. With many others (such as Andrew Murray), the beginning point has been the reality of the individual's prayer life. For myself I must say that in wrestling with this problem about nine years ago in our hayloft in Champéry . . . my own personal point of beginning was the reality of bringing specific sin under the blood of Christ moment by moment, and knowing the reality of forgiveness and a restored relationship. . . .

We are remembering you also, and your family, and the things of which you wrote to us. . . . We do pray for you and long that the Lord will bring something [out of your work].

In the Lamb,
Francis A. Schaeffer

PART II
Spiritual Reality in Daily Living

Resting on the Lord

[To a young woman who became a Christian through Dr. Schaeffer's Bible study classes while a student in Switzerland. Upon returning to her home in England, however, Emily became depressed and began to neglect her spiritual life until her faith grew increasingly unreal and far away. Emily wrote in response to other letters from the Schaeffers, and to express her hopes that the Schaeffers might be able to visit her on their way back to the U.S.]

26th January, 1953   Chalet Bijou
                        Champéry, Switzerland

Dear Emily,

Thank you so much for your recent letter to Mrs. Schaeffer and to me. How happy we were to hear from you and how much we look forward to seeing you. We were unhappy that we had not heard from you for some time, but we have been praying for you that the Lord would keep you close to Himself and help you meet those problems which we were sure you would have.

I am not surprised that you have had difficulties. On the other hand, I am sure that as you stay close to Him—truly so—He will lead and guide you and show you the way in all these matters. When problems arise, our natural tendency indeed is to become discouraged and then to do as you say you did—that is, to neglect all the things of the Lord. This is our natural reaction, and it is only as we grow in spiritual things and rest upon the Lord day by day that we gradually come to that opposite reaction, which should be the Christian's—namely, that as the difficulties arise, we would place these more and more in the Lord's hands and really stay closer to him because of the difficulties. However, I am sure that, since you now feel all your joy in the Lord will return, even these past difficulties will open a new joy in the Lord and service for you.

It is not surprising either that the things of the Lord seemed far away; this is quite a common experience. When we come to the Lord as our Savior and have close fellowship with other Christians—as we all had together in our Bible study classes here and in Nyon—and then we leave such an environment to be plunged into a circle of friends and work where the Lord is never thought of and honored, it is a natural thing in our human weakness that the things of the Lord will retreat until they seem far-off and strange. However, again as we grow in the Lord and stay close to Him, the opposite thing takes place—the things of the Lord become more and more real, and, in the words of the hymn, "the things of earth will grow strangely dim in the light of His glory and grace." . . .

We are looking forward to a time of blessing, and one of the things to which we look forward with the greatest expectation is seeing you again.

Mrs. Schaeffer and the girls send their love to you. Do let us keep in touch with each other, and be sure that we are praying for you.

Cordially yours in Christ,
Francis A. Schaeffer

Sin and Forgiveness

[To a woman who is deeply troubled by sin in her life. Miss VanDoren writes that she has loved the Lord dearly even as a little child, but that as a young woman her spiritual life grew cold. She fell into an intimate physical relationship with a married Christian man. And though it did not come to the place of adultery, she knew this was wrong and is tormented by guilt over her sin. Miss VanDoren longs for peace and forgiveness. She writes to Dr. Schaeffer after hearing him speak. Although she writes concerning a specific situation and a specific kind of sin, Schaeffer does not mention any of the specifics in his response, thereby emphasizing the relevance of the cross and the sufficiency of God's forgiveness for *all* sin whatever it may be.]

December 17, 1953   6117 Lensen Street
                              Phila., Penna.

Dear Miss VanDoren:

Thank you so much for your letter of September 1st. Do not think because I have been so long in answering that you have not been much in my mind, and I have many times held you before the dear Lord's face in prayer. I would have written sooner, but have been traveling much over the country. As a matter of fact, we have just gotten back from an extended trip out to the West Coast and up to the Pacific Northwest. . . .

Your letter touched my heart very closely. I can only say that the wonderful thing is, of course, that regardless of where our feet may have walked, the blood of the Lord Jesus Christ is quite sufficient and enough to care for all these matters. Of course, I think it is overwhelmingly important to realize that sin does block the blessing—whether that sin is in our individual life or in the organization and work in which we are. This being the case, surely we who are in Christian work must first of all be very, very scrupulous in bringing our sin, and the sin of our organization as a whole, under the blood of the Lord Jesus Christ by faith, when those sins occur.

The second thing, I think, is to realize just how horrible sin is in our lives—in yours and in mine and in all born-again Christians'—and thus learn increasingly to flee to the cross when these things come in upon us. My, how easy it is to give in to one weakness or another. And yet how awful it is to consider these things in the light of the terrific cost to God of washing us clean from them—that is, at the cost of the precious blood of the Son of God, shed in His agony in His separation from the Father on Calvary's cross.

As I travel backward and forward across the country, I am increasingly convinced that we who are Bible-believing Christians in the United States are allowing sin to stand in the way of God's outpouring in our lives and in our work. It seems to me indeed that we have put so much emphasis on justification— that is, what occurs when we accept Christ as our Savior the first time—that we forget that as God's people we are called unto holiness, and that the work of the Holy Spirit in our lives and in our work is conditioned upon our commitment to Him. Oh, that we might learn together to love the Lord more and be more committed to His ways.

Thus for yourself I would suggest that you very, very carefully put these things of which you have spoken under the blood of the Lord. And for the future, realizing how heinous sin is in the Christian's life, learn to cry immediately for the power of the finished work of Jesus whenever temptation arrives. I will indeed pray for you to this end, and may God help you and strengthen you every bit in it.

I would ask you too to be praying for us that the Lord would lead us and pray for us in a very special way—for me as I go back to Europe [for five weeks alone], that the Lord may lead and guide and use my time there, short as it is, much for His glory.

I will be happy to hear from you again. I would suggest, if I may, as a point of advice, insofar as you have felt free to write me these things, that now it would be very worthwhile for us to keep in contact one with the other, and that if I can be of further help in any way I would be happy to do so. . . .

May the Lord bless you then, and I will be waiting to hear from you further. The next time I will surely answer you much sooner than I have answered you this time, and I again ask your forgiveness for my answer being so tardy.

Cordially yours in Christ,
Francis A. Schaeffer

A Root Planted in a Garden

[To a former L'Abri student who felt very close to the Schaeffer family. After beginning his Christian life at L'Abri, Jerry traveled to the Far East where his faith became lifeless. The Schaeffers knew of Jerry's struggle and continued to write to him. In response to one of these letters inviting him back to L'Abri, Jerry writes asking if he might indeed "come home" to L'Abri and to the Schaeffers. In his response Dr. Schaeffer uses the striking image of a root lying dormant as an analogy for the working of the Spirit in the Christian's life.]

May 24, 1961   Chalet les Mélèzes
Huémoz sur Ollon, Switzerland

Dear Jerry,

How thankful we are in the Lord for your last two letters. It would be impossible to tell you the joy they have given us— first for yourself as you have been in our minds in all the years that have passed; and second for the encouragement again that indeed "His eye is on the sparrow," and that the work of the Spirit does indeed follow those upon whom the gentle Lord has put His hand to the ends of the earth. What you have written has encouraged us again that indeed the Lord does follow all those who have heard the gospel and have gone away. How wonderful to know that the eyes of the Lord do indeed "run to and fro over all the earth," and to know that no stronghold of Satan is so strong that the living God cannot follow, pierce, and divide asunder.

I thought I should write your letter (rather than Mrs. Schaeffer), for I have a burden on my heart for you. Perhaps you do not remember it, but while you were moving on with the Lord here you brought a root to plant in the garden. You planted it under the pine trees by the gate. As I watched you, I had one of those strange experiences that I have had from time to time in my Christian life. It seemed almost like a merging of yourself and that root. I wondered if it would grow, and I wondered if you would grow.

The root never came up, and you went away, and we did not hear from you for so long. But now, according to the words of the prophet in the Word, God has restored that which the canker worm and locust have eaten in your life. You are alive and flourishing. This is the love of God working in grace and love, and not just [the working of] the natural laws of nature; [this is how] God now works in this world which is abnormal since the Fall.

What I am saying is that since the Fall, all nature is abnormal, but God still works in his common grace to give sunshine and rain to the lost, but still unjudged, world of men. In this natural work of God, when a thing is dead, it is dead, and there is no hope. But it is not so in the spiritual work of God. In this, the love of God transcends all natural expectancies. And you, in your present spiritual life, are a result of that endless and boundless love of God to us—as that which was dead, but which in Christ is now alive.

Now you are alive! But now for God's glory you must grow as the living plant. And as surely as I had that experience on that day of watching you place that plant in the ground, now I would be just as sure that you have unfinished business with the Lord here at L'Abri—to come back to the place where you got off the track, to grow and flourish, to pick up the pieces, and to go on as a keen instrument in the hand of God and of the Spirit.

I never tell anyone that I know what they should do; I always say, "God exists, seek His leading." But in this case, though I would not say I know what the Lord would have you do, it is my overwhelming conviction that [you follow through on your plans] to study with us for a time, and that you now go on from there simply and quietly. . . .

With love in the Lamb,
Francis A. Schaeffer

Sickness and the Attacks of Satan

[To a young married couple who had spent time at L'Abri with their little boy. The husband has recently undergone surgery for cancer.]

December 11, 1962   Chalet les Mélèzes
                              Huémoz sur Ollon, Switzerland
Dear Stan and Gloria:

We were so glad to receive your letter, Gloria, of November 23, and yours, Stan, in December. You were both in our thoughts constantly. It was such a relief to have your letters and be brought up to date about Stan's condition so we could thank the Lord with you for His gentle care. We do thank the Lord that everything went as it did, and it is now our prayer with you that the Lord's hand will remain upon you both as you look forward to these next days and weeks. I am sure that Satan will not allow you to rest as you try to move on in God's things. We do pray that the Lord may strengthen Stan in these days ahead—for his physical well-being in every way, but also that the two of you may have joy before the face of the Lord as you go on together after having passed through this anxious time.

Our trusting the Lord does not mean that there are not times of tears, and I think it is a mistake as Christians to act as though trusting the Lord and tears are not compatible. As a matter of fact, it is my opinion that the greatest trust in the Lord comes when we trust Him in the midst of tears.

Now it is our prayer, however, that the time of tears might be past and that new doors may open before you, as you have walked through this difficult time. On the other hand, we never get to the end of the battle in this life, and it is only as we look forward to Heaven or the coming of the Lord that we can look forward to a time of being absent from battle for any long amount of time. This is the experience we have had in our lives; constantly we are confronted with the wonder of what the Lord does with the poor human resources we place into His hands for His use. And yet with the wonder comes the clash of armor in the constant ebb and flow of the battle. . . .

I well understand too what you said about feeling the presence of Satan so strongly in the waters through which you have gone. He is indeed a terrible enemy. So often, it seems to me, we could not be really sure in our own limited wisdom whether a thing [i.e., an affliction] was from the dear Lord Himself or from Satan. It is wonderful to know, therefore, that we do not have to distinguish totally whether a thing is from the Lord or from Satan. We can simply look to the Lord in love, faith, and trust—telling Him that if He is using us in the midst of the seen and the unseen battle (as in the case of Job), we are willing by His grace; but if it is an attack of Satan, that we do plead the blood of Christ to overcome this enemy of enemies. It is wonderful that we do not have to have absolute knowledge because the Lord does, and we can leave [it up to Him as to whether our affliction is a matter of] His using us in the battle [or of] Satan's attacks, without our having to sort this out in every case.

Of course, we will now be praying that if it is the Lord's will the operation will have completely removed all future and present evidences of cancer. . . .

Now I think I had better stop and say good night to both

of you. . . . . It is late now, and both for [my secretary] and myself I must stop. . . .

Almost everyone here was praying for you both as you went through your especially difficult days. . . .

With warm personal greetings,

In the Lamb,
Francis A. Schaeffer

The Art of Spiritual Growth

[To a young artist who was encouraged by Dr. Schaeffer as a L'Abri student. Randy has recently neglected his own spiritual growth through the distractions of moving and starting art school.]

March 9, 1963   Chalet les Mélèzes
           Huémoz sur Ollon, Switzerland

Dear Randy:

How happy we were to hear from you, though I am afraid you would not know it from the speed with which I have answered you. . . . I do not need to tell you what the work here is like. It has been an extremely busy time indeed. . . .

The weather is turning beautiful now. And though there is snow below us and on the mountains above, yet I have the window open as I am dictating this—a sign that spring has indeed arrived. It is beautiful at the moment, and I am sure you would enjoy it much. . . .

Randy, I do think the only way that our spiritual life does not suffer is to go quite steadily on. It is something like artistic work. So often the pseudo artist is rich in artistic temperament, but has little wealth in regard to going on in a [consistent way.] I remember something I read about Matisse a short while ago. It said that he worked every day regularly. But he made the remark once that the difficulty [with many who wanted to be artists] was that they spent all their time seducing the models rather than painting them.

Well, I think it is something like this in our spiritual life. Because it is the "spiritual area," so many people seem to think it should grow in quite a different way from the normal procedures of life. But this is not true at all, because it is the same God who made the growing of the trees and the growth of our spiritual life. It is intriguing how often Jesus used words from the natural world to speak of spiritual things. And as the plant grows, so our spiritual life must grow. The storms may bend the branches; at times parts are even torn off with the beating of the winds, the snow, and the hail. But growth, as the stem of the plant pushes upward, does follow an orderly procedure.

So it is with our Christian life. If we need to eat regularly, we need to read the Bible regularly. [This is the first element.] It should not become mechanical, but there is no reason why it cannot be done so much every day. It does not have to become sheer "law," but nevertheless there is [a proper balance between] something being just a blind duty and something being done in a totally haphazard manner.

The second element is prayer—learning to have communication with our Father in Heaven. He speaks to us through the Bible most of all; but also, and surely, in other ways. But there must be the communication from our side or the [relationship] is no longer what it was created to be; that is [in terms of our being] moral, rational beings. So regular prayer is very important and would fall into two areas: prayer as I am walking in the street and working with the materials that I work with; and then longer periods of prayer talking to our Father in Heaven.

The third thing is finding a Bible-believing church or Bible-believing group of people and having fellowship with them. This is important too. However, it is better to have fellowship with no one than with someone that calls himself a Christian but in reality pulls us in the other direction.

Then the final thing is speaking to others about the Lord. This is important if others are to know of Christ's saving work; but it is also important for us in our own spiritual life to be willing to commit ourselves anew by speaking to those who do not know about the Lord and all He is, to those who do not know Him. Thus, of course, we are most interested that your spiritual life does go on.

Please greet [your brother] for me and for us. And please also do write soon now, and I will try the next time you write to answer much more promptly!

With love,

> In the crucified,
> yet risen Lamb,
> Francis A. Schaeffer

No Perfect People, Physically or Psychologically

[Some years earlier, Kristina had spent many months at L'Abri, and she and the Schaeffers had been very close. In recent years, however, Kristina had slipped into chronic depression and spent some time in a mental hospital. It was like a prison to her—with no help from a psychiatrist or clergyman, and little contact with the outside world. After being released, she found clerical work, though she continues to live in the cold, grey fog of depression, seldom telling others of her critical needs. Though she was once keenly interested in the arts, she has lost this, along with any interest in religion. In moving to a different apartment, Kristina found several old letters from the Schaeffers which she had never answered, and she was prompted to write. The Schaeffers continued to stay in touch with Kristina and to help her as they were able through her continuing battle with chronic depression.]

July 19, 1963   Chalet les Mélèzes
                                 Huémoz sur Ollon, Switzerland

Dear Kristina:

Thank you so much for your letter of July 2. I cannot tell
you how deeply I was touched by it. I am so sorry that you did
not feel free to write before. You will never know how many
times I have thought of you and wondered where you were. I
have kept you on a special place on my prayer list and have
often really longed for you as I wondered what was happening
to you. I will never forget you in the hospital when I visited you
in _____. I understand too what you write about the difficulty of finding a consolation and reality. I think there are really
two things to see: first, that when a person goes through the
kind of difficulty you have gone through, this kind of feeling is
not to be unexpected; and secondly, all men since the Fall—
although in a far lesser degree and a far lesser agony than you
have known—also have some such problems.

Increasingly I am so aware that just as there are no perfect
people physically, so there are no perfect people psychologically.
There are differences in intensity of physical problems and differences of intensity in psychological problems. But there is no
such thing since man has revolted against God as people who
are completely well, either physically or psychologically. Thus,
as I have people come here who have problems, my own contact with them always involves a very deep realization that
there may be differences of degree and kind of problem, but it
is not that they are sick and I am well. I think this makes for a
depth of human contact that is so lacking in much medical and
psychiatric treatment. So often the doctor stands without a
human contact with those who are before him. But when we
come to one another on a really Christian basis, it seems to me
this need not be the case; rather, we can stand together as poor
people who are marked with the sorrow of a mankind who has
revolted against God.

At the same time, as Christians we do not have to allow

the pendulum to swing between [the extreme of] a false idealism and romantic hope, or the opposite [extreme] of despair. The infinite finished work of Christ upon Calvary's cross not only opens up the gates of Heaven to us when we accept Him as Savior; but it also provides, in the present life, for a substantial advance in the areas of psychological need.

The same thing is true in the areas of sociological need—the communication of man to man on a truly human level. There are no such things as perfect bodies, perfect psychological balance, or perfect communication between men in this world. This must wait until that glad day when Jesus comes back again and our bodies are raised from the dead. But yet, just because there is no perfect balance in the present life, this does not mean that there cannot be substantial advance. What this means will be different in different individual cases. But how thankful I am, in my own problems and in dealing with the problems of so many others, that it is possible, on the basis of the finished work of Christ, not to either have to say foolishly and falsely that all is well (when all is anything but well), or else to simply plunge into the abyss of despair.

Dear Kristina, let us find the way—each in his own way and according to his own need—[to appropriate] the meaning of the work of Christ in our present lives. I have no illusion . . . that you may not simply take this letter and throw it away, and that you could say, what does Mr. Schaeffer know about my sorrows? On the other hand, this is not absolutely so. I too have sorrows in my personal life, in my family, and in the work of L'Abri, as well as in the church at large. Thus, I say to you—let us go on and find that substantial advance which we can know even in this poor present world.

I would say again how much we love you and long to help. . . .

Please do write soon again. With love,

In the Lamb,

Francis A. Schaeffer

Practicing the Work of Christ

[Written in follow-up to a conversation between Dr. Schaeffer
and a conservative Christian seminary professor in the U.S.
The conversation apparently centered on the professor's emphasis upon "mystical feeling" as an essential part of reality in
the Christian life.]

November 20, 1965   Chalet les Mélèzes
                          Huémoz sur Ollon, Switzerland

Dear Bill,

We have just come back to Huémoz a few days ago after
our time in the States and a few days in England.

This will only be a short note, but I did want you to know
that what you said to me [when we last talked together] has
been much on my mind. I do pray for you, that the Lord will
lead you on with clarity.

As I have thought over what I said to you that day, I wish
we could have talked longer. Nevertheless, I think that what I
said must be the basis of the solution for each of us in regard to
reality in our Christian life. Reality does not just come as a
mystical feeling. It comes rather in the whole man knowing the
objective truth of what is, [and knowing this] to be the existence of God and His character of holiness and love.

Then, knowing that this is truth and having accepted
Christ as Savior once for all, it is necessary to practice the
meaning of the work of Christ as a present reality in our daily
lives. This means two things: first of all, claiming the work of
Christ for forgiveness for those specific sins we know we have
committed; and then—through faith, on the basis of the finished work of Christ, and in the power of the Holy Spirit—
looking to Christ, moment by moment, to bear His fruit
through us.

I am convinced that there has been a real weakness in the
Reformed teaching concerning the conscious side of sanctifica-

tion. The Bible surely teaches that we must practice by choice the offering of the work of Christ for our moment by moment forgiveness; and that we must consciously abide in Christ for Him to bear our fruit through us.

I would think that if you could get hold of my "True Spirituality" tapes they would be helpful.

I think that when we come to the place where you said you have come [i.e., to have serious doubts about one's faith], the important thing is to have the courage to ask the same question which we must ask before our conversion—and that is, is Christianity truth? Then, when we know that it is indeed truth, to consciously practice the meaning of the work of Christ in our present life.

I did want you to know that you are in my thinking, and if I can be of any further help, please let me know.

With love in the Lamb,
Francis A. Schaeffer

Waves of Depression

[To Ann, a student at a Christian college and a former student at L'Abri. Ann is in a state of depression, at times crying softly in her bed so as not to disturb anyone. She is afraid of life and wonders if Dr. Schaeffer will share her tears. She wonders too if God is able or if He cares to be involved with the "little people" like herself in an overcrowded weary world.]

December 17, 1967   Chalet les Mélèzes
                     1861 Huémoz sur Ollon, Switzerland
Dear Ann,

I want to write to you immediately. . . . Unhappily, I cannot find for the moment your letter that just arrived. I never lose letters, but I seem to have lost this one for the moment! However, I read it with care and did not want to delay in answering. . . .

I was disturbed by your letter. I do cry with you—and I know the depression, of the moving of the waves, in the ocean of each individual. Unlike the ocean, where the waves are all on the top, the greatest motion of the waves in man since the Fall is not upon the surface but in the depths. This is true for all of us, and especially for all who are sensitive. It is true for all of us, but compounded in some by personal weakness and by personal background—just as others have other kinds of weakness.

It will not do merely to say stop turning inward. This is both cruel and unrealistic. Yet there must be some way to go on, by finding the objective realities of God's existence and the work of Christ in history. With none of us is the way of going on steady or unbroken. But neither must we panic. Nor must we underestimate our subconscious deliberately tempting us—whether the temptations be physical ones or, strange as it may seem, the desire for tears. Nor must we spend a lifetime looking inward—to see what is real in our tensions, and to see what is false and deliberately caused by our [subconscious] selves below the surface. The balance is honesty under the searching of the Holy Spirit; and [at the same time] living in an objective perspective, in the objective realities I have mentioned above.

With sensitivity comes storms; but if the storms are allowed to overcome, the sensitivity becomes destructive rather than the opposite.

You know I am not cruel, but on the other hand, neither can I fail to say that we must not be thankless to God. (I say this, being often thankless myself.) . . . We must also take into account our natural disposition. For example, if we find human relationships vacillating to us, we will almost certainly find the great personal relationship to God vacillating to us. Remember . . . that even in the midst of the storm His promise is true: He holds us fast.

With love in the Lamb,
Francis A. Schaeffer

Beauty and Strength Will Pass

[To Kristina, with whom Dr. Schaeffer kept in contact over
many years (see letter dated July 19, 1963). Kristina wrote to
Dr. Schaeffer after having a vivid dream in which she found
herself in a beautiful landscape enjoying a fine day. But into
her dream there came men dressed in black sheets carrying a
coffin, and Kristina was devastated by how perishable life is.]

March 4, 1968   Chalet les Mélèzes
                       1861 Huémoz sur Ollon, Switzerland
Dear Kristina:
    I received your letter of February 25 yesterday and wanted
to answer you at once. You did not trouble me by talking to me
at the conference—it was quite the other way. I only wish that
we had been able to have more time to talk.
    I was much moved by your dream and the fact that, even
while you were dreaming, you wished to talk to me about it. I
do feel close to you and am glad that I have been able to be of
some help.
    Of course, our perishableness is a trouble to each one of
us. We see the beautiful girl or the athletic boy, and if we have
some wisdom in life we already realize that soon the beauty and
strength will pass. Yet it is just this point where Christianity
does speak with power. As I mentioned to you, Proust, the
French writer, had this thought as the center of his thinking. To
him, death brought the end of all things, and thus "the dust of
death" covers everything in this present life.
    But as Christians we are in a different position. Life does
not end at death. And if we are Christians it not only does not
end at death, but goes on to a thing of beauty. Of course, this
does not remove all the stink of the *present* perishableness, but
it does mean we are not caught. It is for this reason that the
resurrection of Christ is so critical. . . .
    [When I saw you at the conference], the passage I asked

you to read initially was 1 Corinthians 15 [on the resurrection]. With this, you could read what the Bible says in each of the four Gospels concerning the historic event of the resurrection of Christ, and you can also read what the Bible tells us about the future in Heaven from Revelation 21:1—22:5.

There are other passages as well, but I would read these over a number of times: for it is here—in the resurrection of Christ, and in our future resurrection with life going on in an unbroken line—that we have not only a future hope but a present relief. As you know, I am glad that Dr. Hamburger [Kristina's psychiatrist] helps you. But I also realize it is difficult to talk to him about such things. In reality, of course, he too is left naked before our perishableness, especially as he has no Christian hope. This is one reason I think of him so often and wish I could talk to him regularly.

I will not try to write more now, but I did want you to have this at once so that you would have the Bible references I suggested.

I do think of you very often and appreciate your concern for my health. I am sure the Lord does not mean for us to work until we destroy ourselves. But my joy is in seeing many who have such little hope come to the place not only of being saved for eternity, but of being more human in the present life. Please pray for us that we might learn the proper balance of being faithful in what the Lord sends us [to do] and yet not being overwhelmed in matters of health. One thing that is very helpful is that all the members of L'Abri are concerned for us and show much love in their care for us.

We now wait for more news from you.

In the Lamb,
Francis A. Schaeffer

P.S. If you do get here to visit us, we would be glad.

Prayer and the Personal God

[Written to David, a scientist in his early forties, who was raised as a nominal Jew. David became friends with a girl who had studied at L'Abri, and through her he has become interested in Christianity. With his scientific background, however, he has difficulty understanding what really happens when people pray and whether God would hear his prayer. As things are "piling up," he has the growing urge to "pitch the whole thing." David concludes that prayer seems to be his only hope. Dr. Schaeffer's answer explains a number of basic theological concepts which are especially relevant to someone with a probing mind who is testing the truth claims of Christianity. But at the same time, Schaeffer gives a lucid and succinct statement on the nature and operation of prayer.]

April 12, 1968   Chalet les Mélèzes
                      1861 Huémoz sur Ollon, Switzerland
Dear David,

Thank you very much for your letter of April 3rd. It was waiting for me when I returned from a two-week L'Abri Conference in England, and I am writing to you almost at once upon my return. I read all you wrote with great care and deep interest. I am glad that you came in contact with this girl who has been able to discuss Christianity with you in a solid way, and I am glad too that you found the tapes, Bible studies, and my dialogue with Bishop Pike to be of such interest to you.

I only wish we were able to talk, as correspondence is not nearly as good as a give and take conversation. On the question of prayer, I would suggest that you write and borrow a tape from our tape library entitled "Orthodoxy and Prayer." . . .

[In understanding prayer, we need to first understand something about the reality of who God is.] From the Christian viewpoint—and indeed in the Old Testament as well as the New Testament—we must see that God is a personal God. He is infinite and He is personal. Man, according to the New and the

Old Testament, is created in God's image. Thus, though God is infinite and man is finite, yet because man is personal, man was created to be in a personal relationship with this personal God. God created man to communicate through verbalization. Modern anthropology, for example, would say that the characteristic which distinguishes man is primarily that he is a verbalizer.

Since God made man to communicate with other men through verbalization, it is not surprising that there is a place for verbal, propositional communication from God to man and from man to God. The Bible claims (the Old and New Testaments together) that the Bible itself is the verbal communication from God to man. [And in the other direction] prayer is the verbal communication from man to God.

The Bible says further that God created significant history—that is, in contrast to what Eastern religions and modern existentialism teach. [In other words] history is real and significant—like the early modern scientist [believed] in contrast to today's deterministic scientist. The Bible says, however, that *God* is not caught in the machine aspect of the universe which He has made, and that *man* is not caught in the machine either. Thus, from both the Biblical viewpoint and the viewpoint of early modern science . . . man is able by choice to interrupt the machine portion of the universe. For example, when I decide to catch a glass that is falling, I have interrupted the natural law acting upon it. And the Bible says God can do the same.

Thus, from the Biblical viewpoint, when I pray, God does hear and He can act into the cause and effect universe in answer to my prayer. However, God is not a machine. I must not see Him as a vending machine into which I put a quarter and get out a candy bar in a purely mechanical fashion. He is personal, and thus in answering prayer He operates on the basis of what He knows is the best and wisest answer to that prayer, and not just in a mechanical reflex.

I hope this is helpful. As I say, a conversation would be better, and the tape on "Orthodoxy and Prayer" would develop this further. [In regard to your related questions:] I think it is quite clear from the Bible that God does hear children's prayers, though I must say that very frequently the memorized prayer of a child, if that is all he has been taught, degenerates into something like a Tibetan prayer wheel or an act of magic. We never taught our children memorized prayers, but helped them speak to God the way they speak to us.

The New Testament does say that it is the prayer in Christ's name that has the absolute promise to be heard by the Father. This does not mean, however, that in His loving-kindness He does not hear other prayer; and if it has a content in the direction of the prayer that Jesus mentions in Luke 18:13, such a prayer will certainly be heard. This does not mean that one can become a Christian without some knowledge of Christ, but God is infinite and as such knows the cry as well as the action of all men everywhere. . . .

I hope this is helpful and if I can be of any further help, do let me know.

> With warm personal greetings,
> Francis A. Schaeffer

Being Angry at God

[To a young man with a strong feeling of bitterness toward God. Robert has recently been drafted, and this is a primary source of his bitterness. But it is rooted also in a sense of meaninglessness and a feeling of despair over what Robert sees as the cruelties of life and the fact that God does not end these. Robert asked Dr. Schaeffer to write to the army in the hopes that he might be deferred and then come to L'Abri to come to terms one way or another with the God he cannot understand.]

28 August 1969   Chalet les Mélèzes
                              1861 Huémoz sur Ollon, Switzerland
Dear Robert,

Thank you for your two letters. Unfortunately, they arrived when I was away from Huémoz, and so I did not get them until I returned on August 23.

However, as soon as I got your letters I sat down and wrote to your draft board. Whether or not it will do any good I do not know, but insofar as you already have been inducted, I am sure it will do no harm. And let us hope that it does some good. . . .

I am moved for you that you are going through this hard time. Yet I would urge you with all my heart not to allow yourself to be made bitter by these things. I do believe that it would be better for you to have a time here at L'Abri—to get your questions straightened around before you have to go into the service—and I am still hoping this is the way it works out.

On the other hand, if you are drafted, please do remember that the Lord is everywhere. Please also remember that we live in a fallen world, and thus things are abnormal. It is proper to be angry in the midst of this fallen world, but you must be careful to be angry at the right person. It is a very basic part of my own life to constantly remember that Jesus, who claimed to be God, was angry when he stood before the tomb of Lazarus—without being angry at Himself.

In other words, in the midst of a fallen world things are abnormal; they have been changed from that which God made them originally. Christ could be angry at the tomb of Lazarus as He faced the abnormality of death; and we have a right to be angry too. But to be angry at God is both silly and blasphemous. One cannot have the Christian answer that men are really significant in history and then expect God to eradicate every wrong result from that significance while allowing the good aspects of that significance to still operate. If man can influence history, he can influence it for evil and cruelty, as well as for good and noncruelty. . . .

I am still hoping that you can come to L'Abri soon. But if you cannot, I very much do want to keep in touch with you.

                     With warmest
                       personal greetings,
                     Francis A. Schaeffer

Something with Both Usefulness and Beauty

[Some time has passed since Jackie was at L'Abri for a few weeks. Even though her time at L'Abri was so brief, she has corresponded frequently with the Schaeffers and she considers L'Abri her home. At L'Abri she found love and care for herself and for her little daughter, Julie, as well as the beginning of a new life in Christ. Jackie has recently gone through very difficult times and hopes to return soon to L'Abri. Dr. Schaeffer is answering two letters—one written to Edith Schaeffer and the other to a L'Abri worker.]

16 November 1969   Chalet les Mélèzes
                      1861 Huémoz sur Ollon, Switzerland
Dear Jackie,

I have before me your letter of October 19 to Mrs. Schaeffer and your recent letter to Ruth. I have read them both with great, great care. Your letter to Mrs. Schaeffer of course made us very happy, and then your letter to Ruth made us very concerned for you. You must have had such a hard time, and we are sorry.

This will not be a long letter, as Mrs. Schaeffer and I returned home from our trip in America just last Friday night, and I didn't get to read the mail until late last night. In fact I stayed up till two o'clock in the morning to read through all the mail that was waiting, and this included your letter to Ruth. So I cannot write you a long letter at this time, as it is 11:30 on Sunday night, but I do want this to get off to you at once. . . .

I understand that with the problems you faced you felt

very down and, as you said in your letter, *"utterly* rejected." But I would just say to you, please don't feel this way—for first of all the Lord does love you and care for you, and second we love you and care for you and we are now awaiting your coming. As I understand it . . . we are now expecting you about December 1. If I am wrong, pardon me, as I haven't had time to check . . . the reservations list. Anyway, whatever time is arranged, we are waiting for you. . . .

In your letter you say that you have made such a mess of your life. And of course we do have to be fair and say that you have made mistakes which brought you to the place where you now are. I think I must say this, because we must not act as though God has led you (or me, when I have made a mess of things) into that mess. Yet having said that, it does not mean that the Lord does not care for us when we make a mess of our lives, or that He cannot make something beautiful out of them.

Edith has an illustration that I like very much. There was a girl who was supposed to make cakes in the Les Mélèzes kitchen, and she got all messed up until she had nothing but a mess of goo. It would have seemed as though there was nothing to do but throw the whole mess out. But as you know, we don't have a great deal of money, and so Edith has learned to be very economical in the kitchen. Thus she sat down and figured out what was in the gooey mess, and by adding an extra ingredient was able to make it into the most marvelous noodles you have tasted in your life.

Jackie, we often do this with our lives, and then (following the illustration above) perhaps we can't be the cakes we could have been. But if we give ourselves into the hands of the Lord, He can very much reshape us to be something other than we would have been, but something with both usefulness and beauty.

You speak of feeling at times that the only way to end the mess for Sarah and yourself is to end your life and her life.

Don't be too surprised that you feel this way sometimes, for all of us at times feel as though we would like to stop the world and get off, or return to our mother's womb so we would not have to be. I would point out to you that even some of the Bible characters felt this way, such as Job or Elijah. [Indeed it would be wrong if we did] not feel this way at some times in the midst of our own weaknesses and the snares of Satan. But even making the first motion toward putting this into practice [would be completely wrong].

The Lord understands our discouragements, just as He understands Job's and Elijah's discouragements, or Moses' getting mad. What is wrong is: one, to blame God and curse Him; or two, to take any steps toward taking ourselves out of this life. So I was not surprised to read of your feeling overwhelmed with all that has happened to you and all that did happen to you just before you wrote Ruth her letter. But you must not do either of these two things I have numbered above.

Kiss Julie for me, and then kiss her again for Mrs. Schaeffer, and then kiss her for Ruth. And then look in the mirror and know that the Lord loves you just as you are, for you must remember the Good Shepherd knows the sheep by name, including Jackie. And He loved you (and loves you) and He loves me, not on the basis of some romantic projection that we might make of ourselves and which we are not, but just as we are. And as we put our lives in His hands, He is all ready to make those good noodles out of us.

I haven't a clue about the baby's cot [you asked about]. But Ruth is taking this letter in dictation, and I am sure she will look it up and let you know if you have to bring something. We love you, and more important than this, the Lord loves you, so much so that He died for you.

With love in the Lamb,
Francis A. Schaeffer

Psychological Help and the Lord's Resources

[Ken and his wife Cynthia were at L'Abri some years ago. They have young children, but their marriage is a shambles. Ken has all but given up trying to find meaning in his life. Yet he still holds on to a straw of hope that maybe there is some way, with the help of Dr. Schaeffer, to find a measure of beauty and happiness in life and to learn to live with the sad and ugly part.]

16 November 1969   Chalet les Mélèzes
                          1861 Huémoz sur Ollon, Switzerland
Dear Ken,

Thank you for your two letters. The first one was sent to me when I was in the States, where we were for three weeks. The second was waiting for me when I got home this week and went through my mail last night. While we were in the States for the three weeks we were never [very near your area], or I would have tried to be in touch with you.

Of course your letters do bother me, as you already knew they would. You said you wrote the first one while you were drunk, but I am glad you got the address right here in Huémoz, as it did reach me.

I do not need to tell you that I am moved by both of your letters, as I have been by your letters in the past. And I hardly know where to begin in answering you. On one hand my fondness for you and for Cynthia goes on without lessening in any way. And on the other hand, looking back over the years, it is very difficult for me to see where the wrong turn came. My first inclination is to wish that you were near us to see if we couldn't get some of the pieces together again. But then I remember that the last time you both were here in Huémoz we did not get to the bottom of the thing, and so I don't know if we could help now.

There undoubtedly are some people who have been so

affected by the Fall that they need professional psychological help, just as some need a medical doctor. When this is the case it is the right thing to have help, just as it is to have the doctor for a broken leg. Yet without an adequate Christian base it is rather like sweeping something under the rug, or like taking a man apart with the hope that he will go back together again in a better form. But with a Christian base, then I do believe that psychological help at times is necessary. Perhaps in your case and in Cynthia's case this is so. Naturally I have no way to know this from this distance, but perhaps this is the case.

I too feel sorry for your two girls, but this is not my primary sorrow. My primary sorrow is that you have not individually, and then as a couple, been able to have that relationship with the Lord which would open the way for the kind of life that both of you long for individually and as a couple.

I do know, of course, something of the kind of problems you have had with your father and so on, and I am sure a man who is dealing with you on a psychological level will relate to many of your problems. I can believe these things are really not only important, but actually crucial. But having said all this, it is a fact, both in my knowledge and my experience, that merely dealing with such things without a clear Christian base upon which to build is not strong enough. Thus perhaps if you have psychological help it will be a good thing, and I certainly pray this will be the case. And I will be hoping, too, to hear that the man who is working with you has a good balance in the relationship between psychological need and spiritual matters.

We had a good trip in the States, but it was a very tiring one indeed. I must say Edith and I got home very exhausted. I think you know of Edith's back. She has a crushed disk and thus has been having a fair amount of pain from time to time. Naturally this has not helped the tiredness in the pressure of traveling and speaking. On the other hand, we saw many things from the trip which made the work more than worthwhile.

I wonder if the two of you know that Priscilla did have a

baby boy in October. This is the first boy that we have had among the grandchildren. Susan and Deborah are also both pregnant, so if they have their babies we will then have eight grandchildren!

The weather is now changing upon the mountains, with the snow down to just above Villars. The *mélèzes** trees still have their golden color, and though it is getting cold, yet today was a beautiful day indeed.

Do know that I do continue to love you very much indeed. I pray for you, but I don't want you to think of this as simply a "religious" thing, for it is not. It is born out of affection for you before the God who is there. Edith sends her love to both of you, along with my own.

As ever,
Francis A. Schaeffer

* *Mélèzes* is French for larch.

Knowing He Is There Changes Everything

[For the first time in years Brenda is beginning to see some beauty and hope in living. She began to find this with the help of her psychiatrist and through a Christian friend. Some weeks earlier, she had contemplated taking a drug overdose, and had nearly died of an overdose once before. Brenda now finds it "strange but beautiful" to begin to really believe and understand something of God and faith in Christ. And, though she is unmarried, she has taken new delight in her little daughter Kathy.]

6th July 1970   Chalet les Mélèzes
                       1861 Huémoz sur Ollon, Switzerland
Dear Brenda,

Thank you for your letter of June 5. I am sorry not to have answered you before, but in the midst of a very busy life, this has been an even more busy time.

I was so glad that you did write so freely. I am glad that in between your previous letter and this last one you have come to a place of less turmoil. I am glad that you are in the care of a doctor in whom you have a solid confidence. It is most important indeed that we are working with doctors in whom we can have confidence.

I am so glad that during your hard time you did not come to a place of feeling the overwhelming desire to take an overdose of something. I beg of you to sit down and write to me instead, or even phone if that would be a help, if you do feel that way again. There are indeed many reasons why we should go on living, and the largest one is that God really is there, He really does exist, and He made us for Himself. Knowing that He is there, and therefore that we do not live in a silent universe, changes everything. To know that we can speak and that there is Someone who will answer fills the vacuum of life that would otherwise be present. And then, when we realize His love for us as individuals—that Christ really did die for us as individuals, for us personally—life is entirely different.

It is wonderful to know that because He is infinite, He can care for us as though no one else was present in the universe. Because He is infinite, He never gets confused. And as Jesus so beautifully put it, the Good Shepherd knows His sheep by name. We are the very opposite of merely an IBM card to Him.

I am so glad that you are going to be able to go to _____. You did not say when you were going, so perhaps you are there even now.

I was glad to hear that Kathy was doing well. By this time, from what you were saying in your last letter, she must now be _____ old.

We do so very much want to keep in touch with you, and those who have been in contact with you here do not forget you.

With much love,
Francis A. Schaeffer

Imperfection and the Continuing Work of Christ

[To a young woman in her late twenties who has read three of the Schaeffers' books. Sharon has trusted Christ, but is plagued by the recognition of her own imperfection. Although she has tried to find help from her psychologist and her minister, she is still confused. Sharon writes that she does not know exactly what she is asking, but that she hopes Dr. Schaeffer can help.]

26th December 1970   Chalet les Mélèzes
                       1861 Huémoz sur Ollon, Switzerland

Dear Sharon,

Thank you for your letter of December 2. I'm glad you wrote to me, and I do want you to know that I read your letter with much care.

It would seem to me that your central problem, as you have expressed it in your letter, is that you forget the Bible makes clear that none of us will be perfect until Christ comes back again. The Bible states clearly that our standard is perfection: "Be ye perfect as your Father in Heaven is perfect." But on the other hand, the Bible makes equally plain that while this is our standard, yet every Christian has places for further sanctification and growth. The 7th chapter of Romans speaks of Paul's experience *after* he was a Christian. His great cry at the end of that chapter is very similar to your own cry. The difference is that he clearly goes on and claims the work of Christ in . . . forgiveness for his present sin, and thus ends the 8th chapter of Romans with the absolute certainty that nothing can separate us from the work of Christ.

This is where our peace rests—not that we do not sin, but that we can have continuing forgiveness on the basis of Christ's work. This is not to be confused with becoming a Christian (justification). Justification is a once-for-all thing, and we cannot be lost again. The Bible is quite clear at this point.

Sanctification, however, is a continuous thing. [In sanctification, based upon] the finished work of Christ upon the cross, we may have a continuing forgiveness. And gradually, as we allow Christ to do so, He brings forth fruit through us into the poor, external world.

I would strongly urge you to get ahold of my tapes on "True Spirituality"* and listen to them. . . . These studies grew out of my own struggles several years ago at just this point, and I think they will be helpful to you.

Your psychologist is wrong in telling you to let down your high standards, but he is right that these can become an obsession. As a Christian I would say that this may be carried further, for Satan can win a victory in making you feel overwhelmed if you do not see the distinction between the perfect standard of God and the equal emphasis in Scripture that none of us will be perfect until Jesus comes back again.

Christianity is not only a religion for the mentally healthy. Rather, ever since the Fall, none of us are totally mentally healthy, any more than any of us are totally physically well, or totally morally good. Christianity is for weak people just as we are, but we must honor Christ and His finished work by bringing our failures under the work of Christ and leaving them there. When we do less than this, we are dishonoring Christ and His finished work—as though His finished work is enough for some things but not enough for my weaknesses and sin.

We can fail after we are truly Christians because becoming a Christian does not rob us of our true humanity. God does not turn us into puppets which He totally controls just because we are Christians.

I do hope this letter helps, and I do hope that you will get ahold of the "True Spirituality" tapes and go over them carefully.

In reading your letter it is clear that you do have some psychological problems, but this should not be confused with the real matter about which you wrote. And as a matter of fact, if you learn to deal with this, it could lead to less tension psychologically as well.

With much love,

In the Lamb,
Francis A. Schaeffer

* Published later in 1970 as the book *True Spirituality.*

Spiritual Battles Draw Real Blood

[To a Christian who is living in a situation which directly challenges his faith and spiritual growth.]

26th December 1970   Chalet les Mélèzes
1861 Huémoz sur Ollon, Switzerland
Dear Matthew,

Thank you very much for your letter of December 12 which reached me on the 22nd. Thus, I'm writing you just as quickly as I can. I was so glad for your letter, and both Edith and I have read it with very great interest and with prayer for you. . . .

I'm so thankful for your letter and the fact that the Lord has helped you in the midst of your doubts and your pressures. Whether we are . . . newborn Christians or have been Christians for many years, we still have times of battle. Sometimes this wells up out of ourselves because Christians are not perfect and the results of the Fall still influence us. And sometimes, undoubtedly, Satan brings these temptations to us in order to hinder both our bringing glory to God and enjoying God.

We must never forget too that the Bible tells us our actions in the seen world have a cause and effect relationship in the "battle in the heavenlies," in the unseen world.

But spiritual battles must be understood to be real battles

which draw real blood. While the real battle is in the heaven-lies, yet it is never abstracted from life. Satan will always carry the battle into the place of our own problems—whether it is the lack of sufficient money when one is working for a Christian organization, or whether it is the natural longing for . . . person-al and sexual fulfillment. These battles do draw real blood. But we should not be surprised by this, and what matters is, by the grace of God, letting Christ produce His fruit through us—so that in some poor way, and with some incomplete victory, we can find [spiritual] reality in these battles.

It is wonderful, is it not, that what we do does make a difference in the unseen world as well as in the seen world. Yet though it is wonderful, it is also sobering to know that our failures can also make a [destructive] difference in the spiritual battles—[a difference in what happens] between the unseen hosts which have revolted against God their Creator, [as they wage their battle against] the angelic hosts who have remained faithful to God as their Creator and Lord.

Before we're Christians, we are on the wrong "side"; and now, after we're Christians, it is very important that we do not try to serve God in our own strength, but look to the Lord Jesus Christ and to the value of His finished work as He died on the cross for us in space-time history. We look to Him for forgiveness when we've been less than we should be toward our Father, and we look to Him for strength day by day to live a life which praises Him.

Each of us is, in this sense, feminine as a bride, and the Lord Jesus Christ is our Bridegroom. When we take Him as our Savior and then moment by moment put ourselves in His arms, He can and will bring forth *His* fruit through us into this poor world. You were quite right in your letter that it is so very important to ask forgiveness for our individual sins and not just a sort of blanket forgiveness as we tumble into bed at night. . . .

Edith sent you a box of cookies a week ago, and we do hope that you received them in time for Christmas. Do be assured that you're often in our thoughts and in my prayers. I very much want to keep in touch with you. . . . I'll be waiting to hear from you soon.

        With love,

                        In the Lamb,
                        Francis A. Schaeffer

Times of Strength and Times of Weakness

[To Lynn, a student who had spent some time at L'Abri. Dr. Schaeffer continued to be concerned about her spiritual and emotional weakness. But after seeing Lynn later in the year, Schaeffer is encouraged to find that she can "smile again." (See follow-up letter below.)]

4th January 1971   Chalet les Mélèzes
                        1861 Huémoz sur Ollon, Switzerland
Dear Lynn,
        Thank you very much for your letter of December 22 [1970] and for your Christmas card. It was great to see our village church sent by way of [your state]!
        Lynn, how glad I am to have your letter. You have been in my mind far more than you can guess. As a matter of fact I have kept the Joan Baez book [you gave me] in the room here where I see it every day, and in doing so frequently pray for you as it catches my attention.
        We all have our times of being strong and our times of being weak. The swings of the pendulum cover different ground for different ones of us, and the swings of the pendulum are of greater intensity for one of God's children than another. But the swings are there for all of us—for weakness and unhappiness and also for sin. It is for this reason that any honest person must be totally in despair unless they understand the reality of the finished work of Christ upon the cross for us. If it was not

for this, none of us could have any peace of mind either for this world or from the world to come.

The wonder is that when we know God's forgiveness is based upon the infinite value of Christ's finished work, we can then have peace of mind and knowledge of His love, even in the midst of our weakness and depression. And again, we all have depressions too; since the Fall, none of us are psychologically healthy or perfect morally. And I must say that depressions are very hard. This is not unknown to me; though most people do not know it, I have my own periods of depression which are very difficult. I realize that they are not as deep or as often as some people's. . . . But I do understand the depth of feeling that can be involved. But again—and I speak here not from theory but from experience—in the midst of our down times we can know that His arms are about us, and that He does not let us go when our hands are as weak as water.

Thank you for your words. I do want you to know how much you mean to us. . . . Thank you for praying for me. I do have much need for this.

Edith sends her love to you along with my own.

In the Lamb,
Francis A. Schaeffer

[About a year later, written in appreciation for a brief visit while the Schaeffers were traveling near Lynn's home.]

Dear Lynn:

Just a short note to thank you for your lovely letter. I can only say it touched me very much.

The time with you all was really a lovely thing for me personally. I enjoyed those few minutes as much as anything that happened in _____ and I praise the Lord for the time and for you. I'm glad you can smile—glad and thankful.

Do pray for us as we will soon be on our time of vacation—that the Lord can make the results of the time much longer than the time itself. Edith and I are both looking forward to it.

Please give our love to all the others, and Edith sends her special love to you.

In the Lamb,
Francis A. Schaeffer

Cancer and the Sting of An Abnormal World

[To Mary, whose husband Tom is dying of cancer. They had hoped to come to L'Abri, but are having to cancel now since Tom is gravely ill. The doctors say he has no chance to live. Tom graduated from seminary recently with the hope of going into the ministry.]

26th August 1971   Chalet les Mélèzes
                          1861 Huémoz sur Ollon, Switzerland
Dear Tom and Mary:

Mary, your letter of August 19 moved me and all of us at L'Abri very deeply. I must say that Edith and I were really deeply, deeply moved. I have been praying for you, Tom, and for both of you, ever since I heard of your illness, and we too are so sorry that you are not going to be with us.

I do wish I were there to be with you both and to talk and pray with you both. I am sorry that you are in the midst of many conflicting thoughts and emotions. This should not surprise us, for there is a tension in the Bible itself—not because there is a contradiction in it or a tension in the truths that the Bible sets forth; but rather, because of the tension in the world as it now is since the Fall. Since the Fall, we are surrounded by the wonder of God's creation and yet, simultaneously, with the reality of the abnormality of the world and man because of the

Fall. One feels this in the Scriptures and in one's experience, in regard to this life and the next. Thus, we see that to be absent from the body is to be at home with the Lord, and yet that death is an enemy. There is no contradiction in this, but rather a very sharp presentation of the tension between what God meant us to be versus what we are and what death is.

We are praying if it might be the Lord's will that you, Tom, might be spared—both for the battle of our generation and the good of the church, and for the further fulfillment of your life together. But it is also true that unless Christ comes back in our lifetime, the difference for all of us is just that of a very few years.

Yet none of this takes away the sting of abnormality and separation which . . . Jesus knew before the tomb of Lazarus. Jesus, claiming to be fully God, still could be filled with anger standing there without being angry at Himself.

Be assured that Edith and I and the members and workers of L'Abri will be praying for you, and do let us hear further.

With much love to both of you,

In the Lamb,
Francis A. Schaeffer

Do Not Be Afraid to Cry

9 September 1971   Chalet les Mélèzes
                         1861 Huémoz sur Ollon, Switzerland

Dear Mary,

Your telegram just arrived, and we did want to write to you at once. We so much appreciate your telegram so that we can be sharing with you today.

I really am overwhelmingly touched as I think of the fact that you and we so looked forward to your being here. Truly how uncertain are the things in this fallen world. And yet it is wonderful to know that one thing is certain, and this is that the Lord loves us, and that Christ could both weep and be angry at the abnormality of death as He stood before the tomb of Lazarus. It is so profound to think that Christ really could be angry standing there without in any way being angry with Himself as God.

It is a tremendous thing to know that even while the person's body is with us, yet they are already with Christ. Yet it would be totally false to the realities of life not to know also of the sorrow of separation. Even if a person we love was going to be away on a long, long voyage, and we would not see him for a long period of time, we would be lonely. And thus it is not surprising that we are lonely when all communication is cut as it is with the abnormality of death. Do not be afraid to cry—as though this denied your Christian faith. Jesus's tears at Lazarus's tomb indicated the rightness of our crying.

We will be thinking of you, and you must think and pray as to whether it would now be helpful for you to come to L'Abri. Only you can know all that is involved in this, in your thinking and feeling; but from our side, do know that we would certainly find room to have you if you desire to come.

Edith and all of us at L'Abri send our love to you at this time. We do hope that you will keep in touch with us.

With much love in the Lamb,
Francis A. Schaeffer

So We Can Love Him More

[To Vicki, a college student with whom the Schaeffers corresponded for many years. Vicki writes concerning her doubts about God's character and her inability to feel truly sorry to God when she sins. Vicki is also concerned that she is anti-emotional and over-intellectual. She would like to find the proper balance between trusting God in simple, unquestioning faith and using her mind to answer her doubts and questions.]

January 14, 1972   Chalet les Mélèzes
                          1861 Huémoz sur Ollon, Switzerland
Dear Vicki,

Thank you very much for your letter of November 23rd. I was really very glad to hear from you. I am sorry not to have answered you before, but your letter came while Edith and I were in the States for six weeks, and since then I have been snowed under. . . . On the other hand, we continue to see so many things happening that we are filled with thanksgiving as well as feeling as though we are drowning at times. Do keep praying for us that we might find the balance.

When I was in the States . . . I stayed in San Antonio for a physical checkup. They found nothing serious, but they did find evidences of too much wear and tear, and so I am supposed to take it a bit easier for a while. I have changed my schedule, and everyone here in Huémoz has been most helpful, but I must say shifting gears is not easy.

I read all you wrote with a great deal of care. Vicki, when you speak of your stubborn doubts about the character of God and about the Fall, what do you mean? Do you mean that you have intellectual problems at this point? Or do you mean that you simply don't feel as guilty as you know you should feel when we sin? I have come to the conclusion that none of us in our generation feels as guilty about sin as we should or as our forefathers did. I think this basically is the problem of living in a psychologically oriented age. Even though we are Christians, and even though we know there is real guilt, somehow or other we get confused with modern psychological thinking and we don't feel the guilt the way our forefathers did. I am sure that is true of me; and by observations I have concluded that it is true of everybody in our generation—or at least almost everybody.

You need not be afraid to enjoy God. The beautiful thing is that He uses us, but never in the way a soldier would use a gun only to throw it down and take another. He uses us, but He always *fulfills* us at the same time.

In one way I would agree that we cannot reach God with our human reasoning; but in another way, faith is never like a streak of lightning from the sky either. Faith is bowing before God. But I think it's the other way also—namely, that when men stand before God in judgment, He will point out to them that everything in the universe with its form, and everything concerning man with his categories of mind, testifies to the fact that Christianity is the only answer.

Thus, we cannot start with our human reasoning autonomously and have it come out right. But with the open Bible before us, we do not have to park our reason outside the door.

Emotion in Christianity can be right or it can be wrong. We should have emotion as a result of knowing how much God loves us and knowing we belong to him. But the emotion can never be the basis of our faith. The basis of our faith is the content of the Bible; the emotion should be a natural result.

You are surely right that God does not say, "Vicki, you have to go out and learn all there is to know about Me and then worship Me." But He does say that we are to love Him enough to study the Bible to know what He has to say. We shouldn't get caught up in an abstract scholasticism about God, but we do have to love Him enough to find out all we can find out about Him in the Bible so we can love Him more and more. I love my wife—but if I truly love her, then I want to know as much about her as I can. . . .

I have often wondered how you are getting along medically, and I will be waiting for your next letter.

Mrs. Schaeffer and the rest of us . . . send their greetings to you.

With love in the Lamb,
Francis A. Schaeffer

Salvation, Works and Grace, Eternal Security, and the Sacraments

[Salvation—that is, the personal acceptance of Jesus Christ as Lord and Savior—was for Dr. Schaeffer the most important decision in life. Yet Schaeffer stressed that salvation was never merely a "religious experience" in a separate "spiritual" area of life—that salvation does not happen in the abstract or in a "platonic" way. Salvation happens rather when men and women, in the midst of life, recognize their total inability to save themselves—that is, when they recognize their inability on their own to understand life, to know truth and beauty, to have meaning and hope, to find forgiveness, to know who they truly are, and to know their Creator in a personal way. Thus, as we might expect, we do not have many letters dealing with "salvation in the abstract." The vast majority of letters deals rather with how Christian truth and the work of Christ meet *specific* human needs as they confront men and women in the context of daily life.

[Salvation as a general topic is covered most extensively in Schaeffer's book *True Spirituality.* Here Schaeffer writes: "Let me stress it again: salvation is all one piece. All salvation—past, present, and future—has one *base.* That base is not our faith. If we are confused here, we are confused completely. A man can never be justified on the basis of his own faith. Through all of salvation, the only base is the finished work of Jesus Christ on the cross in history." Schaeffer continues that salvation is a unity—"a single piece yet a flowing stream. I become a Christian once for all upon the basis of the finished work of Christ through faith; that is justification. The Christian life, sanctification, operates on the same basis, moment by moment. There is the same base (Christ's work) and the same instrument (faith). The only difference is that one is once for all and the other is moment by moment."*

[In one sense the selections below are not typical of most of Schaeffer's letters in that they tend to deal with salvation in terms of separate topics rather than in terms of salvation in relation to specific personal needs. The following selections have been taken from a number of short letters, usually dealing with only one question, which cover a period of roughly ten years beginning in 1972. Since these letters were often brief and did not usually relate to specific personal circumstances, they have been grouped together here with no attempt being made to identify the recipient and the general situation out of which the letter was written. Together they cover a range of important questions concerning various aspects of salvation.]

December 1972   Chalet les Mélèzes
through December 1982   1861 Huémoz sur Ollon,
                                      Switzerland

Thank you for your recent letter. I wish it were possible for us to talk because it is difficult to be sure one is answering the questions that are really being asked when merely replying to a letter. . . . I do want to do anything I can to help.

The Bible does make plain that we either are a Christian or we are not a Christian—we have either accepted Christ as our Savior or we have not.

• • • • •

Each one of us must say that we are guilty because it was for our sin that Jesus was willing to die on the cross. In a very real way each one of us must say, "I am the one who crucified Christ."

The Bible makes plain that there was no other way that even God could provide a way of salvation except by Jesus paying the price for the guilt of our sin. It is not that He chose this way arbitrarily, but it was the only way which fulfilled the holiness of God and at the same time the love of God. If God had said, "Your sin does not matter, I will accept you anyway," then His holiness would have been destroyed. On the other hand, if He had not provided this way of salvation, His love would have been denied. Thus there was no other way. This was made plain by the fact that just before His crucifixion, when He was in the Garden of Gethsemane, Jesus asked the Father whether there was not another way, and it is indicated that there was not.

• • • • •

I am glad for your emphasis on the sacrificial atonement in your confirmation class. I think the cry of Jesus, "My God, my God, why hast thou forsaken me?" indicated that God in His great love was willing to allow the division which came between God and man in the Fall to be carried up into the Trinity itself and there conquered. Thus most certainly I believe in the substitutionary atonement, but I am sure that when we get to Heaven we will find in addition to this that the atonement is overwhelmingly profound. Without the substitutionary part I think everything is lost, but I am convinced there is much more as well as the substitutionary emphasis. The strongest emphasis ought to be, however, on the substitutionary and propitiatory death of Christ, for without this we have nothing.

• • • • •

As I see it, what the Bible teaches [concerning works and grace] is that we are saved when, by God's grace, we accept the finished work of Christ "plus nothing." This "plus nothing" would include all religious and moral good works. The Bible says, "He that believeth on the Son has everlasting life," and adds no other condition. However, the Bible also makes plain that once we have accepted Christ as our Savior, then, because of our love for Him, we should live in a way that is to His praise. Yet I think the Bible also clearly indicates that none of us are perfect, and thus there will be failures. Therefore, on one hand there should be fruit; yet on the other hand the Bible warns us that it will not be perfect. When we then fail, we are called upon to bring our specific sins under the blood of Christ. And since Christ's death has infinite value because He is God, we may then have a quiet heart that our sins are indeed forgiven.

So on one side the Bible says there should be fruit, and there will be fruit. But on the other hand it says there will be failures which we will need to bring under the blood of Christ. It seems to me this is what the Bible teaches—and there should be no tension between becoming a Christian through faith in Christ the Lamb, and yet being called to a subsequent Christian life.

Lastly, I think the best exegesis of the sin against the Holy Spirit is that it pertains to those who consciously and consistently resist the work of the Holy Spirit, in His drawing power in their lives. This obviously you have not done in your life, and thus you may have a quiet heart at this point.

• • • • •

If we accept Christ as our Savior, the Bible clearly says that Christ continues to hold us fast and that we are sealed by the Holy Spirit. When people "fall away," either they have never really accepted Christ as their Savior, or they are falling away for a time and the Lord will so deal with them that they will return at some time in their lives. Even though one is a true Christian, it is possible to fall away in areas of one's life (such as refusing to accept the authority of Scripture), but our salvation rests upon the finished work of Christ, and thus our sins and discrepancies can be corrected.

We all are weak in faith. But we are not saved upon the strength of our faith, but upon the object [Christ] upon whom our faith is fixed.

• • • • •

There have been two streams of thought in the question you raise about never being lost again. The one is the Arminian stream which would follow Wesley, for example. The other is the Reformed stream, which we must say has largely been the dominant one—though this does not prove, of course, that it is correct, even though it is dominant. This, however, is my view after carefully studying the Bible.

There are two sets of verses in the New Testament. One set warns us very strongly that we must press on to the end. The other verses are those of deep assurance—such as Jesus' assurance in John that nothing is able to take us from His hand or the Father's hand, and Paul's writing at the end of Romans 8 that nothing can separate us from the love of God in Jesus Christ our Lord. And there are other verses of this nature. These verses seem absolute as they are given in the Scriptures, and they do not leave room for anything, including ourselves, to take us out of the Lord's hand.

The verses you presented [Hebrews 6:4-6] and others like them, then, are seen as strong warnings not to take our salvation for granted. But as Paul says in Corinthians, if we build poorly, yet, nevertheless, we are saved though by fire.

One either makes one set of verses normative or the other. And as I say, my own opinion of the Scriptures is that the absolute assurance verses are really absolute. On the other hand, others have had honest differences about this through the centuries. For myself, however, I am quite certain that once we are saved, the infinite value of the work of Christ keeps us fast even from our own failures. Though, of course, this does not mean our failures do not grieve our Lord, nor that He does not chasten us for them.

• • • • •

We must remember that we are new creatures in Christ Jesus, indwelt by the Holy Spirit. And as we are told in Hebrews, the Lord will deal with us in order to bring forth the peaceable fruit of righteousness in our lives. After we are saved, it is not unimportant whether or not we sin. Sin destroys our closeness to the Lord in our lives now; and the Bible does say that Christ will speak to us about our life when we see Him face to face in eternity. The wonderful thing is that because Christ is God, His death has infinite value. And so when we do less than we should (after we are Christians), we can bring each specific sin under the blood of Christ, and it can be forgiven— and our fellowship with him is then totally restored.

• • • • •

I do understand how desperate you feel [that you may have lost your salvation], and I want to do anything I can to help. I think it can best be answered in this way:

The Bible tells us very definitely in John 10 and Romans 8, and in other places, that once we are truly saved we cannot be lost again. We were saved upon the basis of the finished work of Christ and [based on] nothing that we have ever done. Thus, on the basis of the infinite value of Christ's death on the cross, nothing can take us out of His hand or His Father's hand. We are also told that we are sealed by the Holy Spirit, and this seal has all the power of God with it. Thus no person, nor demons, nor the Devil, has power to break God's seal. Therefore, we can have a quiet mind.

On the other hand, the balance is extremely rich in its total content. Thus there are verses that call us to persevere to the end. Both of these sets of verses are important to us. When we have the kind of fear that you have, the first set of verses tells us we may be quiet and trust the Lord's work for us. The other set of verses tells us that we must not become proud or careless—that it is important how we live after we are saved. This does not mean that we will ever be perfect in this life; the Bible makes that plain. At the same time, however, the Bible tells us that after we are saved, it matters that we look to Christ for strength to be overcomers.

I do hope this helps you. I wonder if you have ever read my book *True Spirituality.* If you have not, then I would urge you to get it and read it. I think this would be a real help to you.

Most of all you really should just trust the Lord. After all, He loves us with an overwhelming love, and we should trust that love. I am sure you love your two children and your husband, but the love we have is nothing compared with the dear Lord's love for us.

You really can have a quiet heart.

• • • • •

[Concerning sacraments and salvation], my own view is that salvation is only on the basis of the finished work of Christ and that sacraments should not be added to this, just as nothing else can be added.

• • • • •

I truly am sorry, but I must say that the concept of water baptism being necessary for accepting Christ as Savior really is a return to works. I do believe that as Christians we should have water baptism. But this is a sign and seal of the true baptism which we have when we profess Christ as Savior. As Romans 8 says, if we do not have the Holy Spirit we are none of His. To put water baptism as a necessity for salvation reverses the process and adds works to the finished work of Christ. I feel that the Scripture makes adequately plain that the reception of the Holy Spirit comes when we cast ourselves on the finished work of Christ as He died on the cross for us. Then there should be the water baptism as an outward sign and seal of the inward reality.

• • • • •

It was kind of you to write so thoughtfully to me. . . . In my works [I have not written about the sacraments of baptism** and the Lord's Supper because] I have tried to stay with the more central points rather than getting involved with the less central, since this would then cut off the remarkable way the Lord has used the books, films, and tapes over such a wide spectrum of God's people. This does not mean that these [less central] things are not important or that they are unimportant to me. But I do try to keep them in perspective.

Of course, the Bible does speak positively of water baptism. But as you know, people very close to the Lord have had very different views of what is involved. As I see it, baptism has no part in salvation. If it is made a part of salvation, then we are reopening a new way for salvation—partly on the basis of the work of Christ and partly through works.

However, after we are Christians, we are to obey the commands of Christ. To me, this means belonging to a proper Bible-believing church or fellowship, and also partaking of the sacraments of baptism and the Lord's Supper. As I see it, water baptism should be once-for-all (just as the baptism of the Holy

Spirit is once-for-all), while the Lord's Supper should be partaken many times, since we are to feed upon Christ constantly by faith.

* From *True Spirituality* (Wheaton, Ill.: Tyndale House, 1971), in *The Complete Works of Francis A. Schaeffer,* Vol. 3 (Westchester, Ill.: Crossway Books, 1982), pp. 271, 273. The plan of salvation is outlined specifically in a step by step way and with extensive Scripture references in Schaeffer's little book entitled *Basic Bible Studies* (Wheaton, Ill.: Tyndale House, 1972), in *The Complete Works of Francis A. Schaeffer,* Vol. 2 (Westchester, Ill.: Crossway Books, 1982), pp. 319-370.

** In the early 1950s Dr. Schaeffer did publish a booklet explaining how he understood the Bible's teaching on baptism. This has been out of print now for many years. Schaeffer did not want this brought back into print because, apparently, he did not want this to become a divisive issue which could hinder his ministry as a whole.

The Gospel Is to Give Us Freedom

[To Lisa Berger, a young married woman who has continual doubts and questions concerning the Bible and whether she is a true Christian. Lisa was raised in a Christian family and accepted Christ as a young girl. She reads the Bible regularly, but this only raises more doubts and questions in her mind. She is unable to find any continuing peace of mind and joy in the Lord, and she feels guilty when she tries to enjoy her relationship with her husband and life in general.]

25 October 1974   Chalet les Mélèzes
                              1861 Huémoz, Switzerland

Dear Mrs. Berger:

Thank you for your letter of September 30. I certainly would want to do anything I could to help, but it is difficult through correspondence. I wish we could sit down and talk over a cup of tea for an hour or so.

It does seem to me that you are really caught in a legalism that by God's grace you have got to break out of. The gospel is to give us freedom, not slavery.

God has given us His law in the Bible to show us what His character is. None of us keep it perfectly, and thus we need to accept Christ as our Savior to step from the kingdom of darkness to the kingdom of light. After we are Christians, the law is to show us our standard. But none of us keep it perfectly; and happily when we break it, we can bring the specific sin under the blood of Christ and it is gone forever.

Your section at the top of page 3 shows that you are caught in a real asceticism based on legalism. Christianity should give us a fullness of life in which the whole person is free before God. The idea that anything pleasurable is wrong really misses the point that God made the whole person and God means for the whole person to be fulfilled—not only in Heaven but in the present life.

Thus the Biblical teaching of morality is to be our standard. We are not to add to it, and anyone who tries to bind us with legalisms beyond the Bible is really doing Satan's work and not God's. And we ourselves have missed the way if we bind ourselves with ascetic legalisms beyond the teaching of the Scripture.

Your salvation rests only upon whether you have accepted Christ as your Savior and nothing else. And Jesus is very plain that whosoever will may come.

I would very strongly urge you to get two books of mine and work through them. The first is entitled *Basic Bible Studies,* and the second is my larger book *True Spirituality.* I really urge you to get both and do the Bible Studies first and then read *True Spirituality.* I hope all this is helpful.

With warm personal greetings
in the Lamb,
Francis A. Schaeffer

Things That Will Help Us Grow Closer to God

[To Ellen, a young mother with a baby girl. Ellen wants to become closer to God in a personal way, but she is unable to find the right path to begin. Ellen longs for a feeling of God's presence in her life and wonders if Dr. Schaeffer might be able to help her find the way to becoming personally close to God. She thought that maybe through the "wonderful creation" of having a baby she might become closer to the Creator, but she has not necessarily found this to be the case. She wonders finally whether maybe it is enough just to live for her child and her husband.]

November 3, 1974   Chalet les Mélèzes
                          1861 Huémoz, Switzerland

Dear Ellen,

Thank you for your letter of October 18th. I have read it with much care and really want to do anything I can to help.

There are those things that will help us grow closer to God. The first and most important is a continued and careful living in the Bible. It is not only that we learn facts from the Bible, but it becomes our environment. We are surrounded with a non-Christian environment that constantly separates us from God, and this environment drags us away from God. As we read the Bible and live in it daily, it provides the totally opposite atmosphere—namely, the real reality of the existence of God. There is both the seen and unseen world. And as we live in the total moment by moment reality [of the existence of God and the reality of the unseen world this will help us grow closer to God]. Thus the Bible [as a living environment] is a very central help here.

Secondly, there is prayer. We may think of two kinds of prayer. On one hand, there are rather long periods [which we set aside specifically for] prayer. On the other hand, there is habit of prayer—in the midst of ironing, dish washing, caring for our children—in which we just suddenly speak to God not only of needs, but telling Him we believe Him and the promises He has given us in the Bible about Himself and his care for us.

Thirdly is the matter of talking to other people about Christ. This helps too—for as we tell others about Christ, it helps us to put into words the reality of what we already know about God. This then helps them and us [to see this reality more clearly].

The fourth thing is fellowship with other Christians, and this too is important. When God made Adam, Adam had complete communion with God. Even so, God knew that it was necessary to create Eve so that there would be a horizontal relationship with another human being. Thus, for Christians it is important to have community with other Christians.

The feeling of God does not come first. The feeling of God is the result of our understanding about God from the Scripture, and (as I have written above) the result of our living in the Scriptures day by day.

I do not know that having a baby usually opens the way of closer relationship to God. But having a baby—and then the husband-wife, parent-child relationship—is a help if it is within the framework of living in the Bible, as mentioned above.

Living for one's husband (or wife) and a child is a good and important thing because God has made us this way. However, no finite reference point is good enough, including husband and child. Only the infinite reference point of the personal God Himself can be sufficient. Then these other things have their proper place and beauty.

I wonder if all this is helpful to you. I do hope so, for I was touched by your letter.

> With warm personal greetings
> in the Lamb,
> Francis A. Schaeffer

Do Not Be Afraid of Past Sins Remembered

[To Eleanore, a "student radical" in the 1960s who is now
studying for a degree in nursing. Eleanore's long letter chroni-
cles her radical years—from drugs, to free sex, to terrorist
politics, to Eastern religion. In short, Eleanore tried everything
before making a very clear commitment to Christ. Yet, although Eleanore knows she is saved, her past ideas and actions
often surface in her thoughts, challenging her faith and giving
her a deep sense of grief and guilt. At these times Eleanore
clings to the work of Christ and the basic truths of the gospel
by an act of her will. Eleanore hopes that her experience will
be a warning to others who are attracted by the life she once
led. But more than this, her example and Dr. Schaeffer's response is an encouragement to every Christian who struggles
with guilt and grief over past sins. (Dr. Schaeffer and Eleanore
had corresponded once before.)]

January, 1975   Chalet les Mélèzes
                                       1861 Huémoz, Switzerland
Dear Eleanore:
   Thank you for your recent letter. I am glad that my previous letter was helpful to you. I cannot write a long letter this
time as I just got back from the States and I am drowning in
correspondence, but I did want to write to you without too long
a gap.
   I do want you to know that I read your letter with much
interest, and I was touched by it. I am so glad that the Lord has
led you along as He has. You are so right that when we get
started in non-Christian framework, whether it is in our
thought form or in our life form, we rapidly get into very deep
waters.
   The sixties was a hard time, and of course we here at
L'Abri have seen so many who have been wiped out through
drugs, through Eastern religious thought forms, and through the
promiscuous sex life. Yet we have seen many here whom the
Lord has touched and healed, and we can only be thankful.

On the other hand, it seems to me that with many young people it is even worse now, with apathy ruling everywhere and then not even having the hope of answers.

Coming back to your letter, I do want to say again that it deeply touched me, and I am glad that you felt like writing your history to me. The Lord really is so gentle to us. He certainly makes His promise more than true—that when we ask Him, He is gracious in putting His hand upon us.

Do not be afraid because these things regurgitate in your mind. (I wonder if you have read my book *True Spirituality*? If you have not, I would urge you to do so.) Each time these things come into your mind, bring the specific thing under the blood of Christ and know that, because His death has infinite value, you have a new beginning and can begin again. I too understand your sentence about "willing that you have faith." I really understand that, and I would just say, do not be afraid. On the other hand, be sure to do what I have said—and this is in each case to bring these things under the work of Christ that, on the basis of His finished work, He might forgive you for what is wrong. Then you can have a quiet mind, knowing that whatever [temptation] is left over is a matter of weakness, and by claiming the Lord's promise that He understands because Christ was tempted in every point like as we are, yet without sin.

You are totally right that the greatest test of faith is not the acceptance of Christ for justification, but living like this moment by moment throughout our lives. (As I say, if you have not read *True Spirituality*, please get hold of a copy and read it.) . . .

I am glad you do feel free to write as you did, and would especially say that I will be glad if you would pray for me and for Edith in the midst of our work.

> With warm personal greetings
> in the Lamb,
> Francis A. Schaeffer

Content and Reality in Finding a Church

[To Andrew, a young artist who met Dr. Schaeffer briefly at a conference. Andrew has been directly influenced by Schaeffer's writings on art and culture, and also by the ideas of Schaeffer's colleague Dr. H. R. Rookmaaker. Andrew writes initially to ask if Schaeffer would comment on his art, but Andrew then turns to a long discussion of the problems he and his wife are having in the fundamentalist church where they worship. Although Andrew and his wife have a sincere desire to worship in this church, they have met with little understanding, due to their unconventional appearance and to Andrew's work as an artist, and they have been told not to ask intellectual questions about Christian doctrine. Thus Andrew and his wife feel caught between a desire to worship and minister in the church to which they feel called, and the rejection they feel from the pastor and congregation.]

March 18, 1975   Chalet les Mélèzes
                               1861 Huémoz, Switzerland

Dear Andrew:

Thank you for your long letter, which reached me yesterday. Thank you too for the colored slides of your work and your own picture. I wish I could answer all of your letter at once, but I am in the midst of two months' work on a film and a book. . . . Thus I cannot go into your work at this moment, though I will get to it later. I did think, however, that I should try to answer the other part of your letter [concerning your church] quickly, for I can deeply feel the problem of you and your wife.

The problem you are finding with this church is all too often a prevalent one. Nobody but the Lord Himself can tell your wife and you whether you should continue with this group or not. Thus what I am saying is a general statement which I would urge you to pray over together.

I think we should be in a church that fits into what I wrote in my little booklet called *Two Contents, Two Realities*. (If you do not have this, I would suggest that you get it.) The points in this booklet are: one, the church (or group) should have real Biblical content; two, there should be a reality of giving honest answers to honest questions; three, there should be real spirituality involved; and, four, there should be an orthodoxy of community in the group [i.e., a genuine community of Christian love and caring for one another.]

All too often in evangelical circles there is a strong "platonic" element so that things of the intellect and the proper pleasures of the body are held to be suspect. Fortunately this is better in evangelicalism than it was years ago, and it is a joy to me to know that L'Abri and the books from L'Abri have made a real difference in this in many parts of evangelicalism. Unhappily, however, that does not say that there has been a change everywhere.

My own personal opinion in reading your letter would be that you should try to find a group that touched upon all four points, even if none of them are perfect—as indeed no group or church is perfect in all four or any of these points.

If you do leave, you should leave very gently and without raising crosscurrents in the church. You really must show real love and not feel the need of vindicating yourselves either to those in the group you are leaving or those out of it.

I do hope this is helpful to you because, as I have said, I do feel your problem. I am sorry I cannot go into the art side of your letter, but I am sure you will understand in the light of the pressure that is on me at the moment.

Do greet your wife for me.

With personal greetings
in the Lamb,
Francis A. Schaeffer

Quietness in the Midst of Our Storms

[To Frank, who was at L'Abri some years ago. Frank has been under psychiatric care and is presently in a state of depression.

Although he believes that Christ bore his sins on the cross, Frank has trouble experiencing God's forgiveness in his personal life. Frank writes Dr. Schaeffer hoping that he might be able to help in some way.]

December 19, 1975   Chalet les Mélèzes
                                   1861 Huémoz, Switzerland
Dear Frank:

Thank you for your letter of December 16. I am so glad your letter came today because I'm leaving tomorrow for six weeks [of filming, and I could not have answered you for many weeks if it had come just one day later].

I read your letter and was very touched. I really would want to do anything I could to help you, though I'm not sure what this is except to pray for you, which I do. If you wanted to come to be with [us here], you should write directly to _____. . . . I do not know if a time back here being in one of the L'Abri chalets would be helpful to you or not, but I should think maybe sometime it would be.

We all go through times of ups and downs physically and psychologically, but of course your times of vacillation are greater than, for example, my own. Yet, we must see that each of us goes through these times in some degree since we all are abnormal from the effects of the Fall.

For myself, when I am in a depression, what I do is to turn back to the promises of the Bible and hold on to these. We do have the promise that, because Christ's death on the cross had infinite value, once we accept Christ as Savior He will never let us go.

We also have the promise that as we bring our moment by moment sins under the finished work of Christ, these sins are gone, and we can have a quiet conscience concerning them. Thus, as Christians, we have endless new starts.

Then we also have God's promise that there will be a time

in the future when the marks of the abnormality, in ourselves and in nature, will be completely healed upon the basis of the work of Christ.

Thus whatever my weakness is (whether it be moral, intellectual, physical, or psychological), I do not have to look forward to all my conscious existence being so marked [by the abnormality of the Fall]. There will be a time in the future when the redemption of Christ will cure these things perfectly—just as now, already having accepted Christ as Savior, our true moral guilt has been removed and we are in a relationship with God at this present moment. Thus, on the basis of the work of Christ, we have the present fact that God is now our Father, but we can look to the future for the full redemption of our whole being.

As I've said, we all go up and down, though I realize yours is often profound. Let us pray for each other and go back again and again to the finished work of Christ—for our base and for quietness in the midst of our storms. . . .

Please do be praying for me these next weeks as we shoot the film in the States.

With love in the Lamb,
Francis A. Schaeffer

To Help You Through the Darkness

[To Phillip, a recent graduate from a Christian Bible school who has read a number of Dr. Schaeffer's books. Although he had been a believer for sixteen years, Phillip has decided recently to become an atheist. About a year ago he was diagnosed as having cancer. Phillip says the reasons he decided to reject his faith were primarily the lack of love he found among Christians and the psychological manipulation he experienced from his "liberal evangelical" pastor.]

March 31, 1976   Chalet les Mélèzes
                        1861 Huémoz, Switzerland

Dear Phillip:

Thank you for your letter of March 21, although of course its contents gave me real sorrow for you. I'm overwhelmed for you in the physical sickness that you have. I really am sorry.

We do live in a fallen world—one that is abnormal from that which God has made. Each of us has certain results of this abnormality; each of us has a different mix concerning the way the results of living in this abnormal world affect us. With some it is more physical, with some more psychological, with some more intellectual, and with some more moral. Each of us has some of these, but with each of us certain aspects of the abnormality have a stronger effect upon us than others.

I certainly would do anything I could to help you. Having been a Christian, however, you cannot now be an atheist. You may go through a period of darkness, but once we have accepted Christ as our Savior He has promised to hold us fast forever. Our salvation does not rest upon our holding on to Christ, but upon his work as He died upon the cross. Because He is God, His death has infinite value and can cover every spot. Thus, when He promises to hold us fast and to never let us go, He is doing so upon the basis of the infinite value of His shed blood as He died for us. . . .

You have been in a relationship to this personal God—in the way God Himself has provided through the work of Christ—and as such you can look to Him to help you through the darkness.

You must not lose confidence in God because you lost confidence in your pastor. That is no way to get at the matter at all. If our confidence in God had to depend upon our confidence in any human person, we would be on shifting sand. All of us are weak. All of us make bad mistakes. All of us lack love. All of us are sinners even after we are Christians. I know nothing of your pastor, but regardless of how mistaken he may be (and I know nothing about this), this has nothing to do with God's existence or God's love for you.

I would agree that there are no perfect churches, and if you were here you would find that our congregation is not perfect either. But there is community here, and I wish you could come and share in it. Is there any possibility that you could come and be at L'Abri for a time? I'll enclose a Farel House sheet to tell you the way people come. I do pray for you, and I'm glad you felt free to write.

Warm personal greetings
in the Lamb,
Francis A. Schaeffer

Being Where the Lord Wants Each of Us

[To a young man in his midtwenties who is seeking the Lord's leading in his life.]

September 27, 1976   Chalet les Mélèzes
                          1861 Huémoz, Switzerland
Dear Geoff:

Thank you for your letter of September 11. I am so glad my books have been helpful to you. As you can guess, it isn't easy to write the books in the midst of the L'Abri work. Knowing that the books have been used with people like yourself makes the battle more than worthwhile.

Of course, no one but the Lord Himself can tell you what to do with your life. There is no formula given in the Bible which we may follow mechanically to know the Lord's will. It is a matter of taking one step at a time, as the Lord opens the door before us.

Of course, one thing will always be certain. The Lord's special leading of us will never contradict what He has given in the Bible; He will not deny the absolutes which He has set forth there.

I would be careful of "inner voices." Each thing like this must be judged in the light of the absolutes given in the Scriptures. Inner voices are not always from God, but may actually be from Satan himself or merely the welling up of our subconscious desires. If I were you, I would just go one step at a time and see what the Lord opens up to you.

One thing you should very definitely have in mind—that is that a ministry such as teaching the Bible in a college is no higher calling intrinsically than being a businessman or doing something else. The important thing is to be where the Lord wants each of us individually, and being given into the Lord's hand at each moment and in each place. No one calling is intrinsically higher than another.

> With warm personal greetings
> in the Lamb,
> Francis A. Schaeffer

The Unforgivable Sin

[To Alice, a pastor's wife with two young children. Alice made a profession of faith at eight and, though she has had times of being away from the Lord, she has frequently felt close to Him. Alice knows the Bible well and teaches Sunday school and a Bible study. After reading Mark 3:28-30, however, she became convicted that she had once cursed the Holy Spirit and thereby committed the unpardonable sin of blasphemy against the Holy Spirit. She has confessed this and repented, but she still can find no peace. She writes to Dr. Schaeffer, hoping that he might be able to answer her among the many other letters she knows he receives.]

October 27, 1977   Chalet les Mélèzes
                          1861 Huémoz, Switzerland

Dear Alice:

Thank you for your letter of October 17 which I have read with great care and was deeply touched. I wish I could write at greater length, but literally I am answering this within an hour before I have to leave for work on a new film script. Thus, if this letter seems a bit hurried, please know that this does not mean that I do not feel deeply for you, and that I would not do anything I could to help.

When we examine the passages in the Gospels about the unforgivable sin, it is related to only one thing—that is, to those who say that Christ was doing His work in the power of the Devil. If it was only these passages in the Gospels, then there would really be no problem at all, for this clearly has no relationship to you. However, there is a passage in one of the epistles* which speaks of a sin that is unforgivable and which does seem to broaden it out beyond what the Gospels say.

Yet, in examining the whole of the New Testament, I believe that the answer which has been given by most careful theologians who love the Word of God is the correct one, and the only possible Biblical one—that is, that the sin against the Holy Spirit is *a continual, unending, and constant resistance to the Holy Spirit's work in a person's life* as He would draw them toward salvation.

I would urge you with all my heart to realize that the "proof text" type of study, which we all do in a way, is not really the way to read anything in the Bible. The whole Biblical teaching on any point is always richer than any one single passage. The Bible speaks to us in balances—and it is in the fullness of the total Scripture balance that we have the fullness of God's teaching.

In considering this question of the unforgivable sin in the light of the whole New Testament's teaching, I am certain that the explanation which I gave above is the only one that is Biblical. The unforgivable sin is not something done once for all and which when done is without remedy. It is the constant, unremitting resistance of the gracious work of the Holy Spirit for salvation. This clearly is not your case: what you did was wrong, but is no more wrong than when I and other Christians murmur against God, as we all do. In both your case and mine, the thing should be brought under the blood of Christ, left there, and forgotten—with a "thank you" to the loving Father who sent the loving Son to die that we might have such forgiveness.

Once we bring this or any other sin under the blood of Christ, it is then depreciating the work of Christ to continue to worry about it. His death has infinite value because He is God and covers every sin. Thus, a Christian should have nothing on his conscience. As soon as we know we have sinned, we should bring that specific sin under the blood of Christ. And once it is there, it is dishonoring to the infinite value of the work of Christ to still carry it on our conscience.

I beg you to specifically bring this thing once for all under His finished work; and if, after that, Satan tempts you with worry over it, rebuff Satan by saying in your head or out loud: "Let me alone. That is forgiven on the basis of the work of Christ as He died on the cross."

From your letter I think you would be greatly helped by reading my book, *True Spirituality.* . . .

With warm personal greetings,

In the Lamb,
Francis A. Schaeffer

*This is probably a reference to Hebrews 6:4-6, but see also Hebrews 10:26-31 and 1 John 5:16, 17.

Balance in Choosing a Church

[Dr. Schaeffer was often asked about how a Christian should go about choosing a church. Schaeffer did give specific advice concerning this, and the selections below (taken from a number of letters) provide the basic considerations which Schaeffer found essential in making this choice. But there is another sense in which this advice should not be separated from Schaeffer's work as a whole—as represented by the whole work of L'Abri in its life and community, and by the whole body of Schaeffer's writing. For only in all of this taken together do we see the full scope of Schaeffer's understanding of the church. (See especially *The Church Before the Watching World, The Church at the End of the 20th Century, The Mark of the Christian, True Spirituality,* and *The Great Evangelical Disaster.)* The following selections, then, should be seen as presenting only a small part of the full picture, but nonetheless as providing basic essential criteria from which to begin.]

May 1978   Chalet le Chardonnet
through April 1983   1885 Chesiéres, Switzerland

Thank you for your recent letter. I read all you wrote with much care [concerning your difficulties in finding a church which is truly sound and meets your needs] and I wish I could help. . . .

What group you should be with is something that only the Lord can show you. I would say though that there ought to be three things connected with your choice of a local church or fellowship. First, there should be an "orthodoxy of doctrine"—that is, it should be Bible-believing in the full sense of the term.

Second, there should be an "orthodoxy of community." This means that people would care for each other in the whole spectrum of life, including financially if this is needed. There should be real community among those in the church, and a real sense of the importance of this—rather than the church just being a preaching point or an activity center.

Third, after these two points are met, then you must find a church which meets your personal needs. Theoretically all churches should meet all people's needs, but in a fallen world this is not possible. Some people, for example, like one kind of music and some another; some like one kind of preaching and some another. Some churches meet the needs of certain individuals, but not the needs of others.

However, when you put the three things together, we must recognize that there is no church in this fallen world which is perfect, and unhappily there are an appreciable number of communities where it is difficult to find any church that meets the three criteria.

Two further things must be said simultaneously: first, we must not accept what is poor; second, however, if we will only accept what is perfect or else nothing at all, we will always get the nothing in this fallen and abnormal world. This is true in our personal lives, in our marriages, in our churches, and in everything else. Keeping this balance is one of the most difficult things in the Christian's life, but we must look to the Lord to try to keep the balance.

• • • • •

I think the New Testament does make plain that once we are a Christian we should be in some specific Christian church: this was clearly the practice of the New Testament church. I do not think this is necessary for salvation, but I do think it is a matter of obedience, as is taking the Lord's Supper, for example. However, it is unhappily true that there are many places throughout the world and in the U.S. where it is hard to find a church that meets the three points I have suggested above. In such a case, it may be necessary to join a church some distance away even though one cannot attend regularly. But I do think one should belong to some group as a matter of obedience.

• • • • •

Most of the larger [so-called mainline] Protestant denominations* are almost entirely under the control of liberals in their seminaries and bureaucracies—and their bureaucracies are very strong. This means that there are individual congregations in these denominations that are Bible-believing, but that by-and-large you can be pretty sure even before you go to one of these churches that the pastor will be liberal in his theology at least to some extent. (Incidentally, "liberal" in this sense means that they do not hold the Bible to be the absolute inspired Word of God, and then they go wrong on many other points because of their view of the Bible.)

• • • • •

[Concerning the Roman Catholic Church], the Reformation was far from perfect, and certainly it was no golden age. But it did restore a balance at the point of authority, and on how to be saved. . . . Since Vatican II, as I see it, there are three streams in the Roman Catholic Church: 1) Those who still hold to the things that were believed at the end of the Middle Ages [and prior to the Reformation]; 2) the liberal theologians such as Hans Kung . . . ; and 3) [those influenced by] Vatican II, which suddenly made the Bible more acceptable. [As a result] undoubtedly masses of Roman Catholics have been saved, and I am just so overwhelmingly thankful. Many of these are my friends, and I feel very close to them. But the Church as a church has not changed a lot of its official positions.

• • • • •

On my part, even with the fact that there are some better elements in the Roman Catholic Church (and worse elements as well), I feel very strongly with the Reformation forefathers that the Roman Catholic Church, as a church, is not a true church. . . .

• • • • •

In the area of *religious* cooperation [I personally would have to apply certain limits]. For example, though there are many Roman Catholics who are brothers and sisters in Christ (since they have been reading the Bible after Vatican II), yet I could not cooperate with the Roman Catholics *religiously* on an *organizational level.* This does not mean, however, that I could not have private prayer with them. But I could not have a religious service since this would seem to say that the differences of the Reformation did not matter.

• • • • •

I really could not make your decision for you. Each person must make a choice before the Lord for himself or herself, and then each couple must make their choice for themselves as a couple . . . before the face of the Lord.

*The specific denominational name has been omitted since there is no reason to single out a specific mainline denomination and because the point here would apply equally to other denominations, as Schaeffer has often confirmed.

The Cancer of Sin and the Cancer of Sickness

[To Donna, a young woman who had a close relationship to L'Abri and the Schaeffers some years ago. Dr. Schaeffer heard that Donna had gotten into trouble in a relationship with a man and had made a rather bad mess of things. Schaeffer then wrote a personal letter to Donna, which Donna did not answer immediately since she felt so humiliated by her actions. Finally Donna wrote an introspective letter wondering what she could now do with her life, to which Schaeffer responds as follows.]

January 8, 1979   Chalet les Mélèzes
                                   1861 Huémoz, Switzerland

Dear Donna:

Edith and I have been back in Switzerland for two weeks for the Christmas season [after my time of chemotherapy treatments in Rochester, Minnesota], and among other things I have been going through all the letters [my secretary] has written, and yesterday I came to yours. I am glad she answered you, but because of our closeness in the past . . . and because I have been deeply concerned about you, I did want to write to you directly myself. I do want you to know that I have never forgotten how helpful you were [when you were here in the past].

Of course history is real, and our choices, one way or another, do have a continuing cause and effect relationship in that history. However, having said that, as Christians there is another thing that must be equally said. That is, that we can bring our mistakes and sin under the finished work of Christ existentially, as well as in that once-for-all time when we accept Christ as Savior. When we do this, the guilt of that specific sin which we bring under the work of Christ at any given moment is gone. It does not remove all the results of history; nor does it remove all the scars for us. But it does mean that a Christian should be one who has nothing on his or her conscience. As soon as we have seen where we have missed the way, we should bring it immediately and consciously under the work of Christ. After we have done this, it is then dishonoring to the work of Christ (as though that work were not sufficient) to still carry the feeling of guilt concerning that individual thing.

Again, I would say this does not mean that our choices do not have results in history, nor that we are the same people as if we had not made certain mistakes or certain sins. Yet a Christian is a person who has the possibility of innumerable new starts.

It does not mean that our lives will be exactly the same as they would otherwise have been; and certain things are lost. But always there is the possibility of starting again, looking to God for our help to begin building a fullness of life in the circle of that which we now are. Increasingly I am convinced that this is the secret of living with some satisfaction in this fallen and abnormal world—that is, by realizing who we are at this moment and living to the fullest within the circle of who we are.

It is not always a matter of mistakes and sin. For example, Edith and I are getting older, and on top of that I now have this malignancy.* This is who Edith and I now are. But does this mean that we cannot live a full life? I am not saying that Edith and I do very well in practice; but I can say that with all my mistakes, sin, and now this present sickness, I do find that my life can be full in the circle of who I now am. I would just say that with all my imperfections and weaknesses, and in the midst of this present illness, my life is full. Is it perfect? Far from it. No one's life is perfect in this abnormal world.

I called each of our four children to tell them with my own voice about the malignancy as soon as I knew I had it. Each of the four responded in the same way—that is, by saying . . . how glad they are that I have stressed to them the reality of the Biblical teaching that the world really is abnormal because of the Fall. Thus, they were not taken by surprise, though, of course, there have been tears. Knowing the world is abnormal, and yet knowing that it is possible to bring our mistakes and sin under the work of Christ, means that there is the possibility of living a life, in an unromantic and practical way, that has fullness and beauty—in spite of those scars that are there, either because of our past choices, or simply because of the fallenness of the world.

Thus, Donna, you are wounded—and I really have ached for you as I heard one thing or another along the way. But you are still young (at least you are a lot younger than I!) and there is a life ahead of you—to be lived looking to Christ for your strength within the circle of who Donna now is.

I find it wonderful that we are not what modern man says we are—namely, only determined machines. What a black view that is. Yet every time I consider the wonder of [man's] significance, I am sobered by the responsibility that it brings. Both you and I, in different ways, have seen the sober results of significance in the choices of others and in our own choices.

Yet that which honors the Lord is to bring that which has been wrong under the blood of Christ, and to let Him bring forth beauty in the life that is before us. As a matter of fact, whether it is through poor choices or such a thing as my sickness, it is possible for God to work it for good—in the sense of our being able to show forth the sufficiency of the work of Christ, both before angels and men. And because of the specific experiences each one of us has had as a result of the Fall, each one of us can help others in a way that no one else is able to do. I would say this gently—that my having had cancer has enabled me to be a help to some people that otherwise I never could have helped. The cancer of sin and failure is no different from this, once it is cared for in the Biblical way.

You will be glad to know that my chemotherapy treatments have gone very well, and we need to keep praying; but we also can be thankful. Edith and I return tomorrow to Rochester, Minnesota, and I begin a new series of treatments on the 11th. These treatments should continue until the middle of March, and then we will know where we are. But as I say, so far things have gone well. If you want to write to me in Rochester, my address is _____.

Edith sends her love with my own, and I am so glad you wrote.

In the Lamb,
Francis A. Schaeffer

*Schaeffer was diagnosed as having lymphoma cancer in October of 1978.

Yes, Your Wheelchair Is Welcome

[To Mr. Stephen A. James, a young man confined to a wheelchair after having contracted polio as a child. Although he is from a religious background, Mr. James is not sure what he believes. He writes to Dr. Schaeffer after reading about Franky Schaeffer's polio attack in the book *L'Abri.* Mr. James' polio, as well as the cruelty and evil in the world, have left him with basic questions about life, death, evil, and whether there is a God. He mentions his hope to visit the L'Abri branch in England, which he traced down from references in the book.]

July 24, 1979

Chalet le Chardonnet*
1885 Chesiéres, Switzerland

Dear Mr. James:

Thank you for your letter of July 8. I was deeply touched by it and, as you will see, I am answering you at once. In your letter you said you were going to the Greatham L'Abri on the 19th of July. If you were able to go, and I hope you were, you will have already been there, and I hope you found it helpful. . . .

You ask if your wheelchair will be welcome at L'Abri. The answer is yes, either here or in Greatham. And if you think that it would be helpful to come either here or to Greatham, we would be glad to have you. . . .

We have gone through a number of sicknesses in our family. Franky did have polio, and it was a struggle, although it probably is true that he was not as permanently affected as you were insofar as you are in a wheelchair. When he had it, however, it seemed as though he was going to be extremely handicapped. You would be the one to know the concern this brought.

Then, too, two of our girls have had rheumatic fever—including Susan whom, if you have gone to Greatham, you have probably met. (Susan, with her husband Ranald Macaulay, heads the British L'Abri.) She went through a long period of rheumatic fever, and so did our youngest girl Deborah. Deborah was more affected than Susan, but is able to be very crucially involved in the work here in the Huémoz L'Abri.

Then this past year I was found to have lymphoma cancer, in a very advanced form, and went to Mayo Clinic last October. I did not realize then [that I was very near death]. But after chemotherapy the doctor said that the evidence of malignancy was no longer there. However, I am still having the aftereffects of the chemotherapy.

Why am I saying this? Just simply to say I do understand

something [about serious illness and disability]—not only of the physical aspects, but of the personal ones as well.

It isn't easy, but we must realize that a very crucial part of the Christian teaching is that the world is not the way God made it. We live in an abnormal world caused by man's rebellion against God. And this abnormality involves not only our separation from God, but all the other abnormal things that exist in history now. Thus, many things in history should not have been there and are not the way that God created them originally. Of course, Christ's death opens the way for us to return to God individually. But we are also told in Scripture that one day, on the basis of His death, *all* the abnormality will be removed. In this there is the crucial factor that our bodies will be raised from the dead or, if we are still alive when He comes, changed in the twinkling of an eye.

It is not only cruel and empty-headed to say that it is easy to live in the abnormality of this life, it is also a complete contradiction of what the Bible teaches. Each of us is marred by abnormality in many ways, whether it is physical or otherwise. To think it is easy and not to be overwhelmed at times simply is not what the Bible pictures. (At the moment I am reading the book of Job in my own Bible study. I am so glad this book is in the Bible, for it indicates so graphically that Job did not find it easy, and if we are honest none of us find it easy.)

But it is one thing to say that it is not easy, and quite another to spend our life shaking our fist at what has happened to us. For my cancer—I am sure God did not give me cancer, and it was not and is not easy. But I am also sure that, in a very amazing way, He used my being in Rochester, Minnesota, at Mayo Clinic (where I had never been before) to be useful for many, many people—including many of the doctors at the Clinic.

Thus, there is a balance to find which is not static and once-for-all but moment by moment. I would urge you to get my wife Edith's book *Affliction* and work through it carefully. I

think you would find it a great help, as many other people
have. . . . She did not write this book in a vacuum, but in our
own difficulties, battles, tears—as well as joys—in a part of that
battle which we have known. I really do think the book would
be a great help, and I urge you with all my heart to work
through it.

You say in your letter that you have been told you have a
chip on your shoulder and that you should accept your situation—and that as a young man you cannot do this. It all depends on what is meant: to accept it as normal or God-given?
That would not be according to the Biblical teaching. To accept
it in the sense of understanding that we live in a fallen world
and God hates the sorrows of the world more than we do—even
to the point of sending His Son to die so that eventually there
might be healing? This we should and this we can live with.

The reason that there is such injury in the world, and yet
that God exists, is simply because of the abnormality. It was
man's rebellion against God . . . that brought the abnormality
and that still continues to spew it forth in our society—often,
unhappily, even in our own [lives through our own] choices.

If you are wrestling with the question of whether one may
be intellectually honest and believe in God, I would suggest that
you read my books [starting with] *The God Who Is There*. . . .

I hope all this is helpful, and do believe me that I don't
just write this as a technical response. I can understand something of your wrestlings.

With warm personal greetings,

In the Lamb,

Francis A. Schaeffer

*Although the Schaeffers moved out of the Chalet les Mélèzes in the
village of Huémoz in 1973, they did not begin using their new address at
Chalet le Chardonnet for their return address until 1979. Up until this time
they apparently retained the old address les Mélèzes since this continued to
be the main chalet of the L'Abri work in Switzerland. The Schaeffers' new
home was in the next village (Chesiéres) about a mile up the road from the
rest of L'Abri in Huémoz.

Cancer and the Practical Meaning of the Fall

[To a pastor who is being treated (successfully) for lymphoma cancer. Rev. Logan is interested in starting a ministry to cancer patients and writes to ask Dr. Schaeffer for some comments on his own experience which may be of general help to others who have cancer.]

January 21, 1980   Chalet les Chardonnet
                                    1885 Chesiéres, Switzerland
Dear Rev. Logan:

Thank you for your letter of December 21. . . .

Of course, I was not only interested but touched that you too have begun chemotherapy treatment for lymphoma. I think the ministry that you are trying to carry out is a very needful one, for I have found that those who hear the word *cancer* so often panic and are destroyed by the very word.

I hardly know what I could write that would be very helpful [in a general way] without knowing the individual case involved, since it makes a great deal of difference, of course, as to the kind of cancer and the direction it is taking.

However, in general, I would say that I do not think Christians take the Fall and the present abnormality of the world with practical comprehension and seriousness. I mean by this that although Bible-believing Christians certainly do hold to a historical Fall and the present abnormality of the world as a theological truth, when it comes down to living, this is often forgotten. In other words, we forget that everything is abnormal today, and that much of the sickness in the world and sorrows in other areas are a result of this abnormality. Or to say it another way, there is so much in history that God did not mean to be there, in the way that He created the world and created man.

To me, perhaps the greatest key here is Jesus standing in front of the tomb of Lazarus. The Greek makes plain that He not only wept, but He was angry. In other words, He who was God was angry at the abnormality of death without being angry at Himself. The death of Lazarus, death in general, and sickness come not from God, but flow from the fact that all things are now abnormal.

In forgetting this, Christians, when they hear they have cancer, say, Why did God give me the cancer? This is what I mean by forgetting in practice the existence of the Fall and the present abnormality. I do not believe for a moment that God gave me my lymphoma. It is a result of the abnormal flow of things, just as my eventual death will be from some [abnormal] cause (if Christ does not come back first). This changes everything—for now I can use every medical means, as well as prayer by myself and others, to fight against this abnormal thing that not only I hate, but God does.

In my own case the Lord used Edith's and my time in Rochester, Minnesota, at the Mayo Clinic very richly, and tremendous good has come from this in many lives. Thus, indeed God can use these things in our life, even though He did not send them. But that is very different from being cast in the slough of despondency by thinking God sent this to me. Thus I . . . am not left in the cruel grasp of the thinking [which would say] that if I am sick I either am not a Christian or I do not have sufficient faith. Such teaching is not only wrong but cruel, and it heaps unnecessary guilt feelings on people's heads on top of their illness.

I do believe God can heal either with medicine or without, and more often with a combination of the two. I am so glad that in my theology there is no tension between using the best medicine possible at my point of history, and knowing that God can work directly into my body.

I hope this is helpful. With warm personal greetings,

In the Lamb,

Francis A. Schaeffer

P.S. Incidentally, my lymphoma seemed to have gone away, but now has returned in a mild form and I am on chemotherapy again. None of this changes anything I have written above, but rather puts an exclamation point after it.

What Is a Normal Christian Life?

[To Sally, a married woman with two children in her early thirties. Sally has read many of the Schaeffers' books and has been a Christian for four years. She was raised in a nominally Christian home, but has had a very difficult relationship with her parents. She lives with psychological wounds from this relationship which are frequently aggravated by contacts with her family. At one point more than ten years ago, Sally suffered a nervous breakdown. Sally loves the Lord, but has difficulty finding peace of mind and forgiveness largely due to the past and continuing effect of her family upon her life. Sally wonders whether she can ever have a normal Christian life.]

February 22, 1980   Chalet le Chardonnet
                                     1885 Chesiéres, Switzerland
Dear Sally:

Thank you for your letter of January 18. I read your letter with care and would certainly want to do everything I can to help. It is too bad we cannot talk, for it is difficult to get at a complex matter like this without face to face, backward and forward, communication.

Basically the problem in our own lives, or in the life of our church community, is not to settle for what is poor, and yet to realize that in this fallen world nothing is perfect. Indeed, if we . . . will settle only for that which is perfect or nothing, we will in every case, in this fallen world, end up with nothing. . . .

Of course, having a nervous breakdown complicates the

whole matter, for it is very hard really to separate our psychological problems from our intellectual and spiritual ones. Each thing affects the other, and we all do have psychological problems, including myself—we all do. It is part of the fallen world, and the psychological wounds are as real as the physical ones. I am sorry, though, that you got into the wrong hands when you did have the psychological breakdown. Of course, your pressures in your family, with your parents and sister, have been no help to you in the midst of your psychological problems and spiritual ones as well.

You ask if anyone with such a sick history as yourself can live a normal Christian life. One would have to say, "What is the normal Christian life?" None of us are normal, even after we are Christians—if we mean by that being perfect. What is possible, however, is for us to live in the fullness of life in the circle of who we are, constantly pressing on the border lines to try to take further steps. This is not done in our own strength, but looking to the Lord moment by moment as well as day by day.

I wonder if you have read my book *True Spirituality.* Part of your letter sounded as though you had. If you have not, I would urge you to get it and study it.

From what you said about the various churches you have attended, I cannot tell [you what you should do. What I would say, however is that] we should seek a Bible-believing church which has true community among its people, and which meets our needs on our own intellectual and cultural level—realizing that no church is perfect. I certainly would not say there is such a church in every city, but often we can find one that is helpful to us even though it has great flaws.

Continue to fix yourself, as you wrote, on the fact that once we have accepted Christ as our Savior, we are justified before God on the basis of Christ's atoning work. Do not let yourself be shaken away from this even though at times the waves get high. . . .

If you find it absolutely impossible to be with your family without being wounded, then leave them as much as you can. But if they always wound you, perhaps it would be better only to see them from time to time. . . .

Whether or not you should leave [where you are now living], I do not know. You must find that out for yourself. If the Lord leads you some other place, then it would not be, as you say, "aborting affliction." But you should not run away easily—for, of course, you will go along with yourself. I can understand, though, from what you wrote that you might find it easier to be separated geographically from your parents. Perhaps this might even give you a better relationship with them.

We have [coworkers in your area] that I wish you would look up. . . . They are dear people, and they might be able to be of real help.

I hope all this is helpful to you. With warm personal greetings,

In the Lamb,
Francis A. Schaeffer

God Is Not a God Afar Off

[To Erik Zeller, who misunderstood the teaching of some L'Abri workers on the question of the Lord's will and leading while he was at L'Abri. Erik writes now asking for clarification and for answers that only quote the Bible.]

May 23, 1980   Chalet le Chardonnet
                               1885 Chesiéres, Switzerland
Dear Mr. Zeller:

I have read over your letter most carefully and will do my best to answer. . . .

L'Abri, of course, is interested in holding a truly Biblical position before the Lord and before the teaching of Scripture.

This is important to us beyond all measure. . . . [But when] you ask for only specific Bible passages [as answers], it shows that you come from a much too simplistic thought form. . . . Of course, we all use proof texts, and it is proper to do so. But one should also realize that the Bible is exceedingly rich, and often the full truth of what the Bible teaches is not to be found and enjoyed in merely choosing a verse here and there. It is extremely important to see what the Bible says in the balance of its total teaching—both in didactic statements, and in the way it illustrates what pleases God in the thoughts and actions of His children in their daily lives. This is not to minimize the use of proof texts from time to time. But "proof texting" is not the way to find the richness of what the Bible teaches in its totality from Genesis to Revelation.

Having said these things, and hoping truly that they are helpful to you, I would then state what we would see as the Biblical position [on the Lord's leading].

God is not a God afar off. He is close at hand, and the Bible surely teaches that Christians have an obligation to ask the Lord's will in their walk. In most of their walk they will find that the principles set down in the Scriptures are adequate. As an example, the Bible makes very plain that if I am choosing a wife she should be a Christian. In this particular situation, then, I do not need a special leading of the Lord, but the principles of Scripture tell me the way I should live and walk. A great deal of life is like this.

On the other hand, we come to places where the Bible does not give such a clear indication, and in such cases really we should pray and look to the Lord for His leading. However, it is important to notice that while the Bible indicates this, yet the Bible does not give us any mechanical formula for that leading. One could consider Abraham who was led by both a vision and open communication from God. Moses was led in a number of ways, including the cloud which moved before Israel. But there are also cases in the Scripture where God's people were led in a less specific fashion.

Thus, we should seek the leading of the Lord in the totality of our life, realizing, however, that there is no mechanical formula for finding that leading.

The Lord led my wife and me very clearly in the beginning of L'Abri as set forth in the book *L'Abri*. But this does not mean that He necessarily will lead my wife and myself, nor L'Abri in exactly the same way in other situations. God is a personal God, and it is His freedom to lead us as He wills and not as we dictate.

Having said this, we must then realize that there is a balance to be maintained. . . . [Some have suggested] that leading should always be a sort of streak of lightning from the sky. Of course, God can lead as He wishes, and sometimes the leading is as spectacular as that. But very often His leading is very quiet; and as I have said, in much of life we can lead our lives within the circle of the commands of Scripture.

There are two things to be leaned against simultaneously: the first is living as though God did not exist and as though He could not or would not lead us; the second is living as though God's leading were almost magic without any use of the mind.

Another thing to lean against is [the idea] . . . that we can know God's leading with the same finality that we have concerning the teaching of Scripture, for example, about the deity of Christ. When we are led, we must acknowledge that since we are both finite and sinful we can be mistaken. Thus, the Lord can lead us so clearly [in a particular moment], and yet we can never say at that moment that we personally know this to be truth on the same level as Scripture. When the Lord led my wife and myself to begin L'Abri, the leading was so clear that not to have moved forward would have been disobedience. And yet if you had asked me at that time if I was as sure of this as I was of that which Scripture taught, I could not have said yes. But as the years have passed there is no doubt that we did understand the leading of the Lord [in beginning L'Abri].

Another thing to lean against is the idea that the Lord has a plan for our lives in the sense that if we make a mistake and do not find that plan, then God will devour us and our lives will be a total shambles. This is not so. God is a loving Heavenly Father, and if I make an honest mistake—for example, in choice of a profession—I may be sure that God will gently show me, and I may pick up my life and go on under His loving hand. My life will be different than it otherwise would have been, but that does not mean that it is destroyed. This gives us courage to move forward without fear, trusting our loving Heavenly Father to lead. But if I make a mistake, there will be another way in which the Lord will bless me—in which He will let me serve Him and give me His fullness.

So we must seek the Lord's way for our lives day by day—living carefully within the bounds of Scripture and in constant fellowship with Him so that He would show us our path. Yet I can have quietness in knowing that I may press on without being terrified that I might miss His plan. This is not theoretical. We have had many people come here to L'Abri who have been taught that the Lord leads in a mechanical way, and who fear that if they miss the Lord's way God would devour them. They come here broken from this non-Biblical teaching. And as they realize that God is not a monster—and even if they made an honest mistake God would still love them and care for them—they find freedom and go on with joy, looking for the Lord's leading day by day in their lives.

Thus we face a balance—by living in a personal relationship to God, and by not living as if God were not there. But this does not mean that I must find God's leading in a mechanical and legalistic way, and perfectly in every case, or God will cast me off.

I personally could not live for twenty-four hours without looking to the leading of the Lord, and this is how I live my life, not in theory, but in practice. But I also know the freedom I have of knowing there is no mechanical formula given in the Scripture, but that it must be a day-by-day closeness to God. . . . And I have the freedom of knowing that if I honestly miss the way somewhere, God will still deal with me gently.

I trust this is helpful, and I do hope someday you will come back to L'Abri again. With warm personal greetings,

In the Lamb,

Francis A. Schaeffer

Death Is an Enemy

[To Martha, after the Schaeffers received notice of the death of her husband. Martha and her husband were devout Christians and very close to the Schaeffers. Martha has a young child and feels the loss of her husband deeply. Her faith is firmly grounded in the Lord, but she is struggling on a daily basis to cope with what remains of her life. Her husband died after a long and painful illness.]

August 21, 1980   Chalet le Chardonnet

1885 Chesiéres, Switzerland

Dear Martha:

Thank you so much for your recent letter and for your lovely card. . . .

Your long photocopied letter moved me very, very deeply, and your personal letters perhaps even more. Edith and I think of you often, for we have no illusion that it is easy. Death is an enemy, and God never meant it to exist for human beings. Thus, every death is abnormal. While it is wonderfully true that to be absent from the body is to be home with the Lord, the Bible makes plain that our real hope is that glad day, in the midst of the restoration of all things, when Jesus returns and the total person will be again complete with the body and the spiritual portion. We await that day, for until then all is not complete.

What a delicate balance it is not to see death as less than a present enemy, and yet not to be overcome by the sorrows of death when it comes to a very dear loved one. The balance is not easy, but is the only balance that makes sense in the midst of the world, broken and sorrowing as it is. And yet we are not to be overcome with dark feelings, but to realize that the present has meaning because of the future. It is so easy for Christians to be cruel in telling those that are in profound sorrow of any kind that they should have a fixed smile on their face when really Jesus wept for Lazarus when he died. This is cruel because we should weep—yet the emphasis should be on the total life, and not become a fixation on death. I pray for you for this balance, and I struggle for it before the face of the Lord in my own thinking and life.

I am so glad for all the good things that were written about [your husband]. He really was wonderful, and I love him very deeply. Thank you very specially for sending [a copy of his] last letter. . . .

I read all you wrote about your present life and am glad it is a busy one. I hope all the work in the orchard and so on brings its own kind of fulfillment.

Don't worry about trying to be over-"bright" or about being "under." Just live and be human in the hand of the Lord. And you must not feel guilty because you are still "utterly *désolée"* without [your husband]. This is very natural. . . . Don't push beyond your own strength, and don't feel guilty in finding the balance between your need for rest and your increased openness to people; nor in taking your own path in increasing your outgoingness. This includes backing up sometimes for more rest if it is needed.

I have been at Mayo Clinic on and off for a year and ten months for my chemotherapy. . . . In this time since I have known I have lymphoma [cancer] I have been able to do much work, and I am thankful. Happily, my lymphoma is not giving me pain. I really hurt for [your husband] that this was not his case. The Lord has given us open doors in Rochester, Minnesota, where the Mayo Clinic is—to such an extent that the Christians in the city have asked that we open a L'Abri branch there, to try to be helpful to the Clinic staff, but also with the thousands of patients who come to the Clinic from the ends of the earth. We have done this in buying two houses there and have moved our previous California staff to Rochester. It will also mean that when Edith and I are in Rochester (as I must be from time to time for my treatments) we will be able to carry on L'Abri work there as we do in any other branch—as long as the Lord gives us strength.

As you said your family was "apart" from you, and your Christian friends in _____ are at a distance, do keep in touch with the people at [the L'Abri branch closest to you]. I know that is a long way away too, but they love you and they loved [your husband]—they really did; and I would hope your constant touch with them would be a joy to you. . . .

We count on your continual prayer, and do be assured of our love and care for you. Edith sends her love along with my own.

> In the Lamb,
> Francis A. Schaeffer

Everything Is Spiritual Because God Made Everything

[To Karl Fischer, who has been a Christian for many years but has been under the influence of an extremely strict church group. As a result Mr. Fischer has been unable to find joy in living and a proper relationship between "secular" culture and a "spiritual" life.]

June 25, 1981   Chalet le Chardonnet
                             1885 Chesiéres, Switzerland

Dear Mr. Fischer:

Thank you for your letter which reached here on June 12 and was waiting for me when I got home a few days ago.

Your letter touched me exceedingly, and I want to help you if I can. I think, basically, that unless there is a sufficient basis of truth for our faith, when the winds of adversity come our faith will be blown away. Yet, on the other hand, if our

Christianity is only a bare intellectual system, then again when the winds of adversity come, the certainty of our faith will be blown away. In other words, there must be a sufficient intellectual basis of truth (since Christianity deals with truth), and yet it must not stop only with a bare intellectualism.

Of course, I feel that the group wherein you were led to Christ was mistaken in their "platonic" view of spirituality [i.e., in their total rejection of secular culture and in their emphasis that "full-time Christian service" is the only truly spiritual vocation for a Christian]. There are certain things which are given as absolutely sinful in the Scripture, and these things we as Christians should not do. . . . But then *everything else is spiritual*. The painting of a picture, the work of a good shoemaker, the doctor, the lawyer—all these things are spiritual if they are done within the circle of what is taught in Scripture, looking to the Lord day by day for His help.

Thus everything is spiritual because the Lord made everything, and Christ died to redeem everything. And though full restoration will not come until Christ returns, it is our calling, looking to Christ for help, to try to bring substantial restoration in every area of life.

Of course, we all have fears; but we must learn to really trust the Lord, knowing that He loves us, on the basis of the work of Christ. We are all imperfect intellectually, psychologically, and morally. Yet the Lord does love us, and we do not need to be constantly overcome by fear. That is not to say that we all do not have fear at times. But that is different from constantly living under fear when we have all the promises of the Scripture, not just for the future but for our present day-by-day life. Christianity should give us freedom and not be a straitjacket. Rather than everything being prohibited, everything—except the specifically sinful things which the Scripture names—is in the area of our freedom.

I will try to answer your [list of] questions, though it is not easy within the limits of a letter:

—To be spiritually minded is to realize that we must have

the wisdom God gives in the Scriptures, and not think, as modern man thinks, that his own finite knowledge is a sufficient starting-place.

—You can think about anything [i.e., about every area of life rather than only about a limited "spiritual" area]—as long as you live within the circle of Scripture; that is, by recognizing God's existence and, as God gives you the strength, rejecting what the Bible says is specifically sinful.

—[When the Bible speaks of seeking the things which are above, it is simply saying that we should see] everything from the perspective of God's existence and what is taught in Scripture, rather than seeing things as though man were autonomous; or seeing things as though life consisted only of physical life and death . . . [without taking into account] the totality of reality, which of course includes above all the existence of God.

—In light of this it is perfectly acceptable to study secular subjects, provided they are seen in the proper perspective as I mentioned above. Any secular books may be read, and so on, as long as the individual remains sensitive as to how much he or she can stand. We do not all have the same strengths intellectually or psychologically, and we should not read or see what we really know is too much for us. . . .

—Worldliness is seeing anything in life from a materialistic perspective—that is, from a perspective which makes the material world the final reality, and in which *man's* finite wisdom (rather than Scripture) is everything. In other words, worldliness is removing any area of life or culture from under the judgment of Scripture. . . .

I trust the above is helpful. I wonder if there would be any possibility of your coming to L'Abri here in Switzerland to study for a while. I will put in a Farel House sheet just in case. I do pray that the Lord may help you, for I do understand something of your troubles.

With warm personal greetings,

In the Lamb,
Francis A. Schaeffer

I Believe with All My Heart That the Lord Can Heal

[To Mark, a pastor whose wife, Sharon, has multiple sclerosis. Sharon had spent a number of months at L'Abri years earlier, to decide whether or not God exists. She left L'Abri with a real faith in God and returned home to marry Mark. Recently Mark's ministry and his personal life have been shaken by those in his church who say that God will heal everyone who has sufficient faith, and that the lack of healing is evidence of spiritual weakness. (The letter below includes a few brief comments from related letters written at about the same time.)]

August 2, 1982   Chalet le Chardonnet
                                  1885 Chesiéres, Switzerland

Dear Mark:

Thank you for your letter which arrived recently. . . . We do indeed remember Sharon. I am glad to hear of your life together, and please do give her Edith's and my love. . . .

I do believe that at times the Lord gives direct healing, and I have seen something of this in my own ministry through the years. This is surely to the praise of the Lord, and we thank Him. But there is the constant, pernicious danger of this slipping into the idea that if a person is a true believer and has sufficient faith, he will always be healed. This is clearly *not* what the Bible teaches. The New Testament has various places that show conclusively that not all of the Christians in that day were healed. What this idea does is to forget that God is not a computer but a personal Heavenly Father who must be allowed to answer in His personal and infinite loving wisdom. I have seen some of God's most faithful and loving people wiped out by people telling them that if they are not cured, it is because of lack of spirituality or a lack of prayer. This sometimes certainly is the case, but to tell people who have an acute illness that this is always the case is often to heap guilt on their head when they certainly do not need this.

I believe with all my heart that the Lord can heal any-

thing, but I don't think that He always does. It really is complicated and not simple. As Christians we must know He can heal,
and yet at the same time we must not demand to be healed; and
we must be realistic that what seems to be a complete healing
sometimes proves not to be.

A good example is my own case. When I just found I had
lymphoma, the doctors said I was extremely ill. Six months
later they said they could find no evidence of cancer in my
body anywhere—including the bone marrow where it had previously been very prominent. Literally thousands of people had
been praying for me, and undoubtedly a lot of people felt that I
had been healed. I felt I may have been healed, but I was not
dogmatic about it. And then a year later it was quite clear that I
was not healed; so I went back on chemotherapy and I am
doing exceedingly well. Through all of this I do not think there
has been any pressure on my faith, because although I thought I
may have been healed, I was not dogmatic about it and therefore was not disappointed when later I found that the cancer
had returned.

Thus my own case is clear. I have not been cured of my
cancer. And yet in the three and a half years since I have had
lymphoma, by the grace of God I have been able to do as much
work as I have ever done in my life. I am utterly convinced,
from the letters I receive, that the fact that Francis Schaeffer
has not been "cured" and yet is pressing on in the work has
been a greater encouragement and blessing to hundreds than if I
had been "cured." If I could wave a wand and be rid of my
cancer, of course I would; and I believe the Lord could heal me.
On the other hand, I am perfectly willing to allow Him to be
the judge in these matters. I remain on chemotherapy twelve
days out of every twenty-eight, which is not always easy, but I
can honestly say that I rest in His hands with quietness and
would not change the matter from this.

There is nothing more cruel than a group of people pour-
ing guilt on someone who is ill just when they do not need it.

Thus the teaching that everyone can be healed if they have enough faith is un-Biblical, cruel, and lacking in love. I would repeat, to me this attitude is truly pernicious and un-Christian. I am sure that Sharon with her MS knows what I am talking about.

I am glad that Edith's book *Affliction* has been a help; it is what we believe is Biblical in a total way.

I would think that you should try to rectify this un-Biblical emphasis among those who hold this view in your church. And even with tears it would be better if they left than to destroy the balance of the blessing that the Lord has given you. Then you must personally see what the Lord gives you in this, and after that make your own decision about your ministry. . . .

Edith sends her love to Sharon and to yourself along with my own.

In the Lamb,
Francis A. Schaeffer

PART III

Spiritual Reality in Marriage, Family, and Sexual Relations

Christian Marriage and Sexual Relations

November 25, 1948   Boulevard de la Foret 13
                          Lausanne, Switzerland

Dear Valerie:

Thank you so much for your invitation to your wedding. We truly regret that we cannot be present. It does not seem right that we are so many miles away for such an occasion. If you have a picture taken, we would all like so much to have a copy. We will be remembering you and praying for you. I do wish it were possible to have time for us to talk with both you and Jim before you are married. It is just about impossible to write those things we would like to say.

However, for both of you, don't make the mistake of thinking that there will not be times of stress and strain. This is true in every married couple's life, but in some ways it is especially true of a minister and his wife. I have often felt that in many ways a minister's wife has a harder task than he has. Both must bear the burden of the work, and she must bear the burden of the house as well. It is so easy to get bogged down with duties that there is not time enough to enjoy each other.

We should never forget that marriage is God's plan for us. We should never forget either that the plan of marriage did not come after sin had entered in through man's Fall, but that God made man and woman as they are from the very first. The sexual side of marriage is not a second-best—God meant it from the very first. The Bible clearly teaches this. Thus, the physical side of marriage is to be enjoyed by the Christian. The

175

only thing wrong with that which is sexual is its misuse by the world outside of marriage. God meant the sexual instinct to find its complete fulfillment in marriage. When two born-again Christians stand before God as man and wife, their enjoyment of each other physically is one of the good things of life. First Corinthians 7 is most explicit as a guide for these things. Not to fulfill each other's needs regularly is sinful in God's sight and is putting temptation in the other's way.

This letter is for Jim as well as for yourself. Enclosed you will find a check as our wedding present. We wish it could be much more, but hope it will help in getting started. We will be praying for you in the work as well as your life together. I am sure that the Lord will use you together in a wonderful way in the years to come in [your ministry].

Edith and the children send their love along with my own. With every good wish for the "big day" and for the future,

Cordially yours in Christ,
Francis A. Schaeffer

Marriage Centered on the Lord

January 21, 1949   Boulevard de la Foret 13
Lausanne, Switzerland

Dear Esther:

Mrs. Schaeffer and I thank you for sending us an invitation to your wedding, and thank you too for your Christmas card to us. We know this is a time when you will find your mind and your hands more than full with the many preparations for the time ahead, and we will be remembering you and thinking of you as you look forward to your wedding.

The time when we are married is the most wonderful time in our lives as we begin a new way of life. However, it is also a time when we should be waiting very much on the Lord. To be married to another born-again Christian is a very happy experience, but it is very important that as we begin our new lives together, the husband and the wife have their minds very much fixed on the Lord. Be sure, right from the beginning, to read your Bible and pray together. It is only the home that is centered on the Lord that can be truly happy. Don't wait to begin until later, for it will never be any easier than it is at first.

When we were married, an elderly Christian gave us this advice—"Put Jesus first, each other second, and self last." It has been a good rule for married life.

The Word of God is perfect for every need of life. The physical side of marriage is spoken clearly in the Bible. The Lord has told us that the oneness of the marriage relationship is a good thing which fulfills that instinct which He gave us. In 1 Corinthians 7:1-5 Paul speaks to the Corinthian church to explain to them how sexual sin may be avoided by each man having his own wife. This is how God means for our sexual instincts to be fulfilled. If you will read these verses over several times, you will see how carefully the Lord, through Paul's letter, explains here that the foundation for a marriage, where each is faithful to the other in these things, is based on an understanding that God means each to be careful in fulfilling the other's needs. The Bible, you see, has been way ahead of the modern psychologies; if people had always followed God's Word, they would not have gotten into so many difficulties.

Please give our best wishes to Edwin, and also to your father and mother and aunt. We wish we could be there the day of your wedding, but we hope this will let you know that we will be thinking of you.

Sincerely yours in Christ,
Francis A. Schaeffer

Divorce and Remarriage

[Dr. Schaeffer is writing here to a young couple who are close to the Schaeffers. The question here concerns whether John's brother Peter, who is a Christian, can, in light of what the Scriptures teach, marry a girl who has been divorced.]

June 7, 1957   Chalet les Mélèzes
                                Huémoz sur Ollon, Switzerland
Dear John and Jeanette:

Thank you for your last letter and for the things you sent. . . .

John, for your brother Peter, of course it is hard to give advice this far away. But in general it would seem to me from what you said that there would be no Scriptural reason why Peter shouldn't marry the girl. But his personal feelings are another thing in the matter. If I were he, I would simply tell the girl very frankly that I was going to take time to think it over and take time to look into the case. If she is showing good faith in this she shouldn't mind that, and she should give him the details that would enable him to go over the legal record. Reading the legal record might give him a key as to what his feelings in the matter really are, and it would surely show him if there is any blame on the girl.

As far as Scripture is concerned, my personal feeling increasingly is in the opposite direction from the way many fundamental men seem to be going. My feeling increasingly is that the older Protestant position allowing for two reasons for divorce is correct: 1) adultery on the part of the other; and 2) desertion in its correct sense. Increasingly I feel that it is wrong to conceive of God binding the innocent party for life in either of the two above cases. Thus, if the girl's husband deserted her, and if all possible reconciliation has been refused to her, and especially if he has married, then I would personally feel that Scripturally Peter could marry her. That does not mean that he must, but that he should feel at liberty to think and pray about the matter.

I must frankly say that as I get older I personally wouldn't feel a repulsion to marry a woman just because she had been married before. It is fine to marry a woman who is a virgin if she is the one the Lord directs you to. But I don't think the emphasis on marrying a virgin should become so great that the thought of marrying anyone else is less than best. The girl certainly should be told that if she has really taken Christ as Savior the Lord has forgiven her for her past mistake, if she made a mistake, and it has been put under the blood of Christ. The blood of Christ covers anything. If I can be of any further help let me know, and do let me know how it turns out. . . .

Do continue to pray for us here. We feel much the need. Among other things, last month's finances were very low. Pray with us that this month's may be higher.

We send our love to both of you,

Francis A. Schaeffer

Dating—Christians and Non-Christians

[To a former L'Abri student and new Christian concerning his relationship to his Christian girlfriend, and concerning the question of whether Christians may ever date non-Christians.]

[December 1957]   Chalet les Mélèzes
                                   Huémoz sur Ollon, Switzerland
Dear Jim:

Thank you for your long letter. It was such a joy to Mrs. Schaeffer and myself and all of us to receive. How thankful we are to know that you are coming on spiritually, and to know that you did find the Lord here at L'Abri. We do rejoice now to hear from you after so many months and to hear how wonderfully you have gone on with the Lord in this recent time. We will be thinking about Cynthia and yourself and will be praying for you both, that the Lord may show you clearly what He wants your relationship together to be. Go slowly until you are very sure, and, Jim, be careful that you both look to the Lord for His strength so as to not allow physical things to press you on more quickly than the Lord would have you go. You can be sure that if you do want the Lord's will concerning Cynthia, the Lord will make it plain to you.

Concerning the question of dating non-Christians, the following is what we would say: it depends upon why a person is dating a non-Christian. I feel it is always wrong to date non-Christians with any possibility in mind of marrying them. You must remember that the Bible says clearly that we are not to marry a non-Christian. And to be a realist, one must recognize that we marry whom we know, and whom we go with. And at some point, if we are going with someone steadily and enjoying their company, physical attractions begin and these can be very powerful. On the other hand, if a Christian occasionally takes out a non-Christian, and does not just carry on small talk, but uses the time to sit somewhere in a tearoom, drugstore, or restaurant, and talk directly about the things of the Lord, that could be a different matter.

A lot would depend on what you mean by a "date." Surely in such a case there should be no holding hands or anything that would put it on that basis, but only a serious conversational type of friendship—with the Christian having predetermined that it would be absolutely nothing more.

I hope this is some help to you. I don't think it is the kind of thing you can make an absolute rule about. The individual must determine why he is doing this and what he really is doing, before the face of the Lord.

We will be very happy to hear about your time at the Inter-Varsity meeting in Urbana. And we do praise the Lord for what you wrote about your mother. If you see Ed Phillips give him our greetings. We all send our love in the Lord,

                                        Francis A. Schaeffer

The Marriage Ceremony and Sexual Relations

November 22, 1962   Chalet les Mélèzes
                              Huémoz sur Ollon, Switzerland

Dear Reinhart:

I cannot tell you how happy we were to receive your letter. My response was quite undignified, for my response was: "Three cheers!" Really we were happy to hear from you, and I look back on my conversations with you with really deep interest and pleasure. I must say thinking over your emphasis on the fact that so many people just believe on the authority of human beings has rung a bell in my own mind. I realized this for many years. However, the way you said it has put it in a very clear way in my thinking, and this has been very helpful.

However, most of all we want you to know we are thankful that you found help here, in opening the doors toward a personal relationship through Christ to the God who is really there. Thus your letter was a pleasure to us in both directions. At the same time I want to thank you for the photograph you enclosed. We really are very fond of _____ and we are glad for the picture. Please greet him for me.

Reinhart, you are welcome any time you want to come. We just hope that your visit can be fairly soon. . . .

[Concerning] your question, there is no answer directly to your question in the Bible, for the question is not asked. It would be easier to talk about this, but I'll try to give an answer and if it is incomplete we can talk about it when we see each other.

Marriage in the Bible is not centrally a marriage ceremony. It is interesting that while it is clear that the Jews had a marriage ceremony at the time of Christ, and that Jesus put His complete stamp of approval upon this by attending, yet nevertheless in neither the Old or the New Testament is a specific form for a marriage ceremony given. Marriage from the Biblical viewpoint is when a man and woman stand before God and declare that they are married and then go on and have sexual relationship. This does not mean that the marriage ceremony should be minimized at all; it is quite the other way. The marriage ceremony is overwhelmingly important because, since man is a sinner, man lies and cheats. Therefore, because man lies and cheats, the church and society must protect itself by having a specific ceremony in which the declaration before God is made.

But note that marriage is the declaration before God and then sexual relationship, and not centrally a declaration merely before men either in the state or the church. However, such a definite point must be held or (man what he is) it would be all too easy to have sexual relationship and then to excuse it, and then to walk away from each other using the words of the Bible that speak of the adulterous woman as "she wipes her lips and says she has done no evil."

On the other hand, think of a situation where two Christians would be shipwrecked on a desert island. They are both Christians, and neither are married. Consequently they are free to marry each other. In such a case they do not need to live on the same desert island in agony, while being in love with each other, until rescued. They could simply kneel down and declare their marriage before God who would hear them, and then go on to have sexual relations. They would be married.

Therefore, it would seem to me that the answer to your question falls into two parts. For the sake of the testimony of the church, and in the light of first what men would think and secondly because of our own weaknesses, Christians should not have the sexual relationship before the marriage day. On the other hand, this should be separated from the absolute thing—this being that marriage is basically a vow before God (and not men) and then sexual relationship. I wonder if this answers your question? . . .

Reinhart, we live in a day when the world is on fire. Such

a man as yourself, if you accept Christ as your Savior and truly and really give your life into the Lord's hands, can surely be used in the battle that rages through the world today, and surely through [your country]. May the Lord lead you to that place and make you such a man for Him.

In the Lamb,
Francis A. Schaeffer

Sexual Relationship Before Marriage

[Jennifer wrote to Dr. Schaeffer first to share her deep sorrow over her brother's rejection of the "infinite personal Christian God" and his acceptance of irrationalism and a vague Eastern mysticism. The main part of Jennifer's letter concerns her relationship with Dan, a Christian whom she met at L'Abri two years earlier. Jennifer's concern is that Dan has slipped into moral relativism, especially in the area of premarital sex. He likens sex to a wrapped Christmas present which may be opened only at Christmas. But Dan can't think of any good reason for this rule. He objects to having his hands slapped for "handling the package before Christmas." Jennifer is confused about what the Scriptures really teach and writes to Dr. Schaeffer asking for his counsel and prayers. Jennifer is an outstanding philosophy student planning for graduate study at a leading university.]

December 19, 1965   Chalet les Mélèzes

Huémoz sur Ollon, Switzerland

Dear Jennifer:

Thank you for your letter. I was especially glad that you wrote immediately upon receiving your brother's letter to you. I have not been able to answer before, and in fact I am dictating this on a Sunday afternoon. And yet this does not mean that I have not thought much about you and your brother since receiving your letter.

I can understand both your crying and your anger. There is a place for tears and there is a place for that anger, as long as both are in their place and as long as the anger is directed at the proper object.

As you can guess, my whole reaction is to wish that I could speak to your brother. Of course, it is not that I can help everyone by any means, but I do wish I could talk to him and try. . . .

As far as the problem that Dan raises, I would point out that it is not true from a Christian position that sexually one's hands are slapped even when you touch one parcel. It is a matter of things being at the right place at the right time. First, *there is no possible reason* that one must wait to be married until after graduating from graduate school. Secondly, there is no reason to think Biblically that there could be *no* proper man-woman relationships prior to marriage. Anyone except the naive can see some kind of boy-girl relationship, even in the little boy pulling the little girl's hair. It may not be kind, but on the other hand it would not necessarily be sinful. Later there are the boy-girl conversations, and later the holding of a hand. All these have their place, and none of them are sinful in their place. Then when a boy and a girl decide they belong to each other, a process begins—and there is no law against this process proceeding at a proper rate. As one passes the point of engagement, others things fall within the proper relationship. The question is simply that the timing is correct—and that is that sexual intercourse arrive with marriage. Thus there are lots of things [in the relationship] which are like touching the package and feeling its shape and its size.

On the other hand, it is not merely an arbitrary thing that sexual intercourse is shut up to marriage. I have thought about it for many years, and I am convinced that this prohibition from God is one of God's good gifts to us for two reasons. First, we all are sinners and cannot trust ourselves no matter who we are. We are not married until we are married. And it is all too

easy to leave one partner brokenhearted if full sexual relationship has been taken and later the other walks away. Secondly, I
am convinced from long consideration and observation that it
is really beautiful for us to know the mannishness of the man
and the womannishness of woman in one person. And I am
convinced that the man and the woman who keep themselves
physically only for the one, really know more about the full
mannishness and the full womannishness than those who have
sexual relationship with many or with a number. One knows
more about the average of a limited number of bodies if one
has many [sexual relationships], but I am convinced one knows
more of man and woman as a whole entity by shutting up the
whole interplay to one [partner].

I trust that what I have just said about this makes clear
what I mean. It would take longer than I am able to write now
to develop this; but I trust the above is clear and not confused.
Also, sexual hunger is different than hunger for food. Its *fulfillment* is related to personal interchange, and not just to [an
individual act like] eating—even if [one means eating] ever so
politely and then wiping one's mouth and walking away. This
proves not to be fulfillment.

For the non-Christian, however, in one way we can say
that it is right that there is no reason not to have full sexual
relationship before marriage. But if one is going to say this, one
must be consistent and also say that for the non-Christian,
then, there is no reason not to murder. From the Christian
viewpoint, there is a reason in both cases. First, there will be a
judgment which will balance the books. But there is a second
reason. God has given us these rules not because He is arbitrary,
but because the rules he has given us are fixed in His own
character. And He has created man according to His own character. Thus the rules and what man is conform. Thus, when we
sin we break the law of God, but at the same time it is in the
direction of destroying what we really are. . . .

Finally, many psychologists are agreeing that girls as a

whole simply cannot take sexual looseness. This is not only because it is the girl who has the baby, but psychologically as well, many are coming to say this. In other words, as in all things that go against God's commandments and what He has made us to be, it is the weak one who is injured. That which is wrong always injures the weak one, and so the sin is compounded.

I hope all this is helpful. I have already written much, and so I will simply say for the rest that I am glad for those things which are encouraging you. The Lord did seem to use our time in the States in a very special way.

In the Lamb,
Francis A. Schaeffer

Divorce and Remarriage

[Mr. Preston rejected Christianity in his youth largely due to the immoral actions of two ministers. He went on to become highly educated in psychology, philosophy, and social psychology. After nine years of a "crippling marriage," he was divorced and lost all hope and meaning in life. At this point Mr. Preston met a committed Christian girl and began to carefully reconsider his beliefs, though he cannot honestly say that he is a Christian yet. Mr. Preston would like to marry the girl, and although she shares this desire, she believes it would be wrong to marry him because he is divorced. If it is indeed wrong, Mr. Preston does not want to marry, but his hope is that he can in fact marry the girl without thereby committing the sin of adultery. Mr. Preston writes apologizing to Dr. Schaeffer for imposing on him by seeking his advice in this matter. But because of his "sympathy for some of Dr. Schaeffer's views," he values his personal counsel, and hopes to be able to visit Dr. Schaeffer in Switzerland with the girl he wishes to marry.]

November 14, 1966   Santa Barbara, California

Dear Mr. Preston:

Your letter was forwarded to me here in California. I am in the United States for a few weeks lecturing.

I would wish that you would be able to visit us in Switzerland to talk over these matters—especially if the two of you could be there together. It is difficult in a letter, and especially in a rushed time as is the case in the midst of my lecture period at this time, to deal with your question carefully. However, I will try.

From my understanding of the Scripture, I believe that the general Reformation view is the correct one. As I see it, the Scripture does indicate that there are two grounds for Biblical divorce and remarriage. If you have access to a Westminster Confession of Faith you could pursue in it the Reformation position as given in that Creed. This is, that in the case of adultery or in the case of desertion which cannot be healed (and especially if the one who walks away is a non-Christian walking away from a Christian), the individual then has the right for divorce and for remarriage. (I realize that the Church of England has taken a different position, but I think that from the Scripture it is mistaken.)

Then, of course, in your case there is a very clear added factor of someone who goes through a divorce and then later becomes a Christian. It would seem to me that in such a case the blood of Christ covers this sin as well as any other. Thus from my viewpoint, in such a case as your own, after one becomes a Christian he should try to reestablish his past marriage if this is possible. However, if it proves truly to be impossible, which could be the case for several reasons, then he has a right to choose a Christian wife and begin again—just as a man who commits a different sin has a right when he becomes a

Christian to count the past under the blood of Christ and to begin afresh.

Of course, it is difficult for me to apply this to your individual case because I do not know you, but the above is the principle as I see it from the Scripture. If you were here, I would talk to you about your original marriage and why it broke up. I would also ask you if it were possible or not to try to reestablish your past marriage. If, however, it was not possible to reestablish your past marriage and all other things being equal and right in the Lord, it would not seem to me that you were shut out from considering this present marriage that you desire.

If we were talking together, I would also talk to you quite clearly as to whether you are a true Christian. This, it seems to me, would be crucial to discuss and be certain of.

I would suggest three possibilities [for us to meet and talk together]. . . .

I trust this is helpful. Most of all I wish that you and the girl could spend some days with us in Switzerland, to spend some time quietly before the Lord in considering these things together.

With warm personal greetings,
Francis A. Schaeffer

Marrying a Non-Christian

July 12, 1967   Chalet les Mélèzes
                                     Huémoz sur Ollon, Switzerland

Dear Arlene:

Your letter arrived today and though this is a very busy time, as we are in the middle of an Arts Festival Week, yet I felt I should answer you at once.

I read all you wrote with great care. Arlene, on the basis of the Bible's clear teaching, I can only write one thing to you.

That does not mean that I write it in a cold fashion at all, nor, on the other hand, that the Lord cannot change the situation. However, it is clear from the Scriptures that Christians are not to marry anyone except true Christians. Thus the concept of marrying and then each worshiping God in his own way cuts across that which the Bible clearly teaches.

I have dealt with people for many years, and it is not only that the Scripture clearly teaches this, but my pastoral experience emphasizes it as well. If the man will not consider the claims of Christ as Savior, and actually come to decide [to become a Christian] during the time that he wishes to marry the girl, it is an overwhelmingly unusual thing if he ever will come to such a conclusion after he has the girl.

This in no way says that I do not really think it is awfully hard, especially when our heart is already involved, to hold to a Scriptural position carefully. But I am convinced—not only from Scripture, but from experience—that to do otherwise is not only wrong, but almost always filled with tragedy. . . .

On top of this is the fact that someone who comes from a Mohammedan culture, and continues in Islam, tends to be one person when he is studying in England, but then he tends to be something slightly different when he takes his wife back home into the Islamic culture.

It is my advice from long experience that even when the man is a Christian, if possible, the girl should see him at home in his own culture before committing her whole life into his hands. This, however, is a very secondary point in comparison to the absolute command in Scripture not to marry anyone but a Christian.

Let me say also that it is very difficult for a girl to make a careful decision, and a courageous one on the basis of Scriptural teaching, after she is in love. This is especially true if the girl is a bit older and has these drives and forces in herself which are so overwhelming and almost frightening in their strength— when she begins to fear, though she may not admit it even to herself, that she may not be married. This which I write is difficult for you I'm sure, but it's the only thing I could write—both on the basis of the Bible's teaching and past experience.

On the other hand, God can change things and thus indeed you are both welcome here at L'Abri if you wish to come. . . . Do be assured that we would do all we could to help, and perhaps, in the providence of the Lord, your friend might become a true Christian, and then you could go on without a problem in this regard.

> With warm personal greetings
> in the Lamb,
> Francis A. Schaeffer

Marriage—Putting Christ First

May 20, 1968   Chalet les Mélèzes
                               Huémoz sur Ollon, Switzerland

Dear Hansfried and Olga:

Thank you very much for your wedding announcement. Mrs. Schaeffer and I and all of us at L'Abri do wish to send you our warm greetings on this day of your wedding. We hope it will be a joyous day in every way.

However, as you also know, we will be praying for you that the wedding day itself will be the beginning of a married life to be lived before the face of the Lord. Marriage is wonderful, but unless both are children of God through faith in Christ, and unless both put Christ first as Lord in their lives, then a marriage can never be what the Lord meant marriage to be. This would always be true, but it is doubly true in a day such as our own which is so filled with confusion and tensions. It is only when each one puts Christ first that there can be a sufficient base.

And though at first it might seem as though this would be disruptive to a marriage—to have even Christ put before the other one—yet it is not this way. This is so because, if we put Christ before the other person, we will then be able to love and be thoughtful of the other person in a way that would not be possible if that person was put first.

We do pray for you, that as you begin your home it will indeed be a home which will speak for the Lord in a clear way in the midst of the many upheavals through which our generation is passing.

Everyone here sends their love to you, and Mrs. Schaeffer and I do in a special way.

With much love,
Francis A. Schaeffer

Premarital Sexual Relations and Christian Responsibility

[Linda, who is an unmarried young woman, recently recommitted her life to Christ and found a vital, new spiritual reality while at L'Abri. She writes now with concern about what responsibility she has to a Christian young man with whom she had sexual relations before her recommitment. She wonders whether she is in fact bound to him in marriage before God because of her past relationship with him. But also she wonders how she should regard a later sexual relationship with another man. Linda wants only to do what is right and what is the will of the Lord. But she feels torn. The young man cares for Linda deeply, but she is unsure of her own feelings and whether they really are suited to each other.]

June 28, 1968   Chalet les Mélèzes
                                 Huémoz sur Ollon, Switzerland
Dear Linda:

Thank you for your letter of June 13. I was very touched by it. . . .

[Concerning your question], I would have to eventually say that you must find for yourself what the Lord wants for your life. It would seem to me, however, that since you have had sexual intercourse with _____, and he loves you, that you must give him every possibility for marriage. I do not think the intercourse you have had with someone else after this obliterates what I have said about [your responsibility to the first man]—any more than if a Christian woman after she has married is tempted and sleeps with another man. In such a case, she is not "unmarried," but must tell the Lord she is sorry and go back and pick up the pieces. Also, I think that there can sometimes be other circumstances which enter in so that having intercourse is not to be considered as being binding. For example, if this boy had married somebody else, it would be over. But as he is a Christian and still loves you, it would seem that you must give him his opportunity.

You will remember the three overlapping circles that we use in regard to marriage [the spiritual, the intellectual, and the physical]. It would seem that the spiritual one is in place. The questions you raise, as to whether you share a common view of life and cultural and intellectual interests, would have to be weighed and presented quite openly together. I would suggest a practical starting-point would be getting my two books [*Escape From Reason* and *The God Who Is There*] and reading them with him out loud and talking about them. I really would suggest doing this. Perhaps you will find that this opens the door more quickly than you expect. . . .

I would not push off too lightly this responsibility and possibility. If you have a home of your own and a stable marriage, it could easily open the way for the possibility of doing what you really want to do for the Lord. Finally, I would end where I began—and that is by saying, of course you eventually must know the Lord's way for you. But the above is what I think is Biblical plus what I could visualize *might* be the Lord's way for your life and for your joy.

Do pray for us as the summer crowds are upon us. Fortunately, I am feeling well and I am thankful. You do mean a great deal to us, and Edith sends her love to you with my own.

In the Lamb,
Francis A. Schaeffer

Homosexuality

[This carefully developed letter was written by Dr. Schaeffer in response to a letter from Hans, a European pastor. Hans' questions arise out of his contacts with homosexuals, and in response to the views of some pastors he knows who say homosexual relations can be quite acceptable under some circumstances, and that the Bible only speaks against certain kinds of "wrong homosexual feelings." Dr. Schaeffer felt some urgency to respond since Hans knew of six homosexuals who had recently committed suicide.]

August 11, 1968   Chalet les Mélèzes
                           Huémoz sur Ollon, Switzerland
Dear Hans,

Thank you for your letter of February 20. I am sorry not to have answered you at the time, but this has been an overwhelmingly busy time. I will simply answer the questions you asked.

Homosexuality and lesbianism are growing by leaps and bounds. Of course there have always been these practices. But now that society is becoming permissive about them, some who otherwise might have felt tempted, but who would have not entered into open practice, now easily fall into the practice of the thing. It is, of course, all a part of our present post-Christian relativism.

I prefer to use two words: homophile and homosexual (or lesbian). By definition, to be a homophile is a person who is born so that they have a natural tendency towards affection and sexual practice with their own sex. The homosexual or lesbian is the person who practices this. Not all homophiles practice homosexuality, and not all those who practice homosexuality were born homophiles.*

There are two mistakes that can be made. The first is to fall into the modern relativism that would say homosexual practice is not wrong—in the same way that they would say heterosexual relationships outside of marriage are not wrong. The thought behind both of these is the same: that the Bible is not counted as an absolute, and what nature decrees is right. In other words, no account is taken of the Fall.

The opposite mistake is the one that the orthodox people have made. That is, that homophile tendencies are sin in themselves, even if there is no homosexual practice. Therefore the homophile tends to be pushed out of human life (and especially orthodox church life) even if he does not practice homosexuality. This, I believe, is both cruel and wrong. We who are heterosexual have sexual temptations which we do not give in to by the grace of God. The homophile may have temptations which he does not give in to by the grace of God. And, if this is so, then in neither case should it be called sin.

There are those with homosexual tendencies who can be cured, and happily we have seen a number of cases here at L'Abri involving both men and women.

In approaching these people it is imperative that we do not compromise our Christian absolutes—that is, that we say what the Bible says, which is that homosexual *practice* is wrong. But it is equally important that they feel within themselves that we do not count ourselves better than they. To say it another way, their sins are no greater than our sins.

If a person who has homophile tendencies, or even has practiced homosexuality, is helped in a deep way, then they may marry. On the other hand, there are a certain number of cases who are real homophiles. In this case they must face the dilemma of a life lived without sexual fulfillment. We may cry with them concerning this, but we must not let the self-pity get too deep, because the unmarried girl who has strong sexual desires, and no one asks her to marry, has the same problem. In both cases this is surely a part of the abnormality of the fallen world. And in both cases what is needed is people's understanding while the church, in compassion and understanding, helps the individual in every way possible.

My guess would be that the twenty-nine-year-old woman you mentioned who is married is a real homophile, and, on a Christian basis, now that she is married, she would simply have to find her way with her husband so that he may have what he needs in sexual intercourse and yet understand her problem.

Incidentally, I feel that if a man or a woman leaves their husband or wife for homosexual practice, it is equal to what I believe the Bible teaches in relationship to heterosexual unfaithfulness—namely, that heterosexual unfaithfulness gives a right for divorce and remarriage on the part of the innocent party.

It is sometimes said that the Bible only speaks against homosexuality in relationship to pagan worship, but this is not true. It is quite clear that the Bible says any homosexual practice is wrong, just as any heterosexual relationship outside of marriage is wrong.

Of course we must have compassion. But this is no reason for moving from the Bible's absolutes into the modern permissive society. It is my own experience that if one deals with compassion, one can say it is wrong without people being driven to suicide.

As to homosexuals saying that they can practice homosexuality while praying together, I can believe that some Christians have. But I also know that some people have committed adultery together in a heterosexual relationship and would say they have done the same thing. The answer is that we live in an abnormal world and all kinds of things do exist, but this does not make them right.

I hope this is helpful. Please greet Anna for me. The members of L'Abri need your prayers to have wisdom in knowing what is the Lord's will for L'Abri as so many doors are open to us.

With love in the Lamb,
Francis A. Schaeffer

*It should be noted that Dr. Schaeffer's thinking on homosexuality did undergo some change in emphasis between what is stated in this letter and what we find in later letters (compare this letter with others in Part Three dated January 3, 1979; August 4, 1980; and August 28, 1980). Schaeffer always maintained the distinction between the homophile (someone *born* with a homosexual tendency), and the homosexual (someone who *practices* homosexuality). Likewise he always maintained that many (or probably most) homosexuals are not born as such, but have acquired the tendency; and that homosexual *practice* is always sin whether practiced by the homophile or by the person with an acquired homosexual tendency. The shift we see in Schaeffer's treatment of the subject is toward less discussion of whether a person is a homophile, while maintaining his emphasis upon the sinfulness of all homosexual practice. This shift in emphasis may be related to the rise of homosexual advocates who have tried to justify homosexual practice on the grounds that they were born as a homophile. This position was always unacceptable to Schaeffer without qualification on Biblical grounds.

The Meaning of Love—The "Spiritual" and the Erotic

[Written to a young man in Japan (Moto) who had broken off his relationship with an American woman (Carolyn) whom he deeply loved. The couple had been considering marriage, but the relationship fell apart because Moto doubted that his love for Carolyn was pure enough and sufficiently "spiritual," and because he was afraid that his love was spoiled by his erotic feelings for her. The couple was close to the Schaeffers and had spent time together at L'Abri. Moto had apparently left a number of Dr. Schaeffer's previous letters unanswered.]

July 4, 1970   Chalet les Mélèzes
                           Huémoz sur Ollon, Switzerland

Dear Moto,

I have received both of your letters, and the one of June 28 arrived just this morning. I do want to answer you at once. I do feel very close to you and feel that in some ways I may speak to you as a spiritual father. I trust you do not mind if I say exactly what I think.

First, I do love you and am most anxious that this matter with Carolyn does not spoil your spiritual life—either for your own growth and joy, or for your service to the Lord. I am sure that if you stay close to the Lord He does mean to use you. And even though I weep for you in your personal sorrow, yet I can believe that out of this can come a better perspective which will enable you to be more certainly of service in the name of the Lord in the midst of this poor wounded generation in which we live.

I would have written to you along these same lines previously if you had answered my letters. I am not chiding you for not answering, but simply saying that I did not write previously as I am going to write now because you did not answer my letters, for it is my policy never to force myself on anyone, even if they are my natural children or my spiritual ones. I strongly feel that one of the great curses of much of evangelical Christianity is people feeling they have a right to tell other people what the will of the Lord is for them; and frankly I feel that some of your mistake has its origin in what I think was poor advice to you by Christians since your return to Japan.

If standards are raised which are not really Scriptural, and especially if these are put forth as the spiritual standard for which we should strive, it can only lead to sorrow. If we try to have a spirituality higher than the Bible sets forth, it will always turn out to be lower. I realize that Christians who do this do not think they are setting forth a standard different from the Scriptures, but in reality it is this.

[In the area of the love relationship as in all of life], there are two dangers which must be resisted. The first is antinomianism. This has been a heresy from the early days of the church. Antinomianism teaches that since we are saved by the blood of Christ plus nothing, therefore after we are saved it does not matter how we live. The opposite danger, which is just as destructive, is any form of asceticism. Asceticism is the devaluation of the whole man—theoretically to enhance the spiritual portion of man. This devaluation of the whole man can be the devaluation of the intellect, the artistic, or the physical. What men forget is that God made the whole man, and no part of man is inherently sinful. Each of the parts of man can be sinful, and in a fallen world, even for Christians, there is no perfection in this life in any portion of our lives.

Thus two things are involved. The realization that we are never perfect in any part of our life means that we must continually bring our failure in any part of our life under the blood of Christ for forgiveness. And at the same time we must ask Christ to bring forth His fruit in all parts of our life. The other thing we must constantly keep in mind is the fact that there is no part of the whole man that is intrinsically sinful in itself. The idea that the "spiritual" is high while the intellectual or physical is low is not Biblical Christianity. It is an asceticism born out of the imposition of platonic thinking upon Christianity. I must say, from your letters to Carolyn and now your letters to me, it would seem to me that you have fallen prey to this mistake. There are two elements in your letter which indicate this: first, your emphasis on selfless love and second, what you wrote about the erotic.

The Bible tells us to love our neighbor *as ourselves.* We have a right to love ourselves and even a duty to do so, because we have been made with value, as God Himself made us in His own image. In a sinful world this rapidly can become egoistic and cruel, but that is because we are in a sinful world and not because loving oneself is wrong. Of course we must not love ourselves above God, or even above our fellowmen, but we have a right to understand that there is a proper love of oneself.

In a love affair therefore between a man and a woman, to think that we should only *give,* and that we have no right to ever *take,* is both wrong theologically and romantically in a totally bad sense. We must not exploit the woman: but we have a right to have pleasure and take from the relationship, as well as give. We have no right to make her a plaything: but if the love is to be valid, both take as well as both give.

As for the erotic, this too in a fallen world (and even among Christians) can become sinful, but it is not sinful in itself. To try to build a man-woman relationship and to separate the proper physical sexuality from the total complexity of the relationship, is exactly contrary to the way God has made us and therefore how He expects us to be. We love the whole woman and not a part of the woman; nor do we break her up in pieces in our relationship. We do not love her, and then in some ashamed way have sexual intercourse with her. The man loves the woman, and the woman loves the man; and in the man-woman relationship this includes sexual intercourse. This is the way God meant it to be. It is not that there is something high and holy and pure in the area of the spirit, and that the other is just a biological necessity in order to have children. It is that God made us, and God's statement to Adam and Eve was that they were to be one flesh. Anything less than this is sub-Biblical and sub-spiritual. Anything less than this is some variant of asceticism and eventually destructive.

It seems to me that you have spent your time in an agony which is in itself wrong: both in the area of seeking a selfless love and in the area of seeking a sexless love. I do not know if you came to this mistake by yourself or if you received it from someone after you left here, who in the name of spirituality gave you something both unrealistic and un-Biblical.

As I said, if you had answered my letters I would have written this way to you before, but I did not want to force myself upon you when you did not answer. Now I would tell you that we continue to love you, and it is our prayer for you that you will go on with the Lord. These mistakes have contributed to your losing Carolyn. This I am sure is irrevocable, but it does not mean that God will not give you another. But I beseech you in the name of the Lord that when God presents to you another woman, that the next time you do not make these mistakes. Even if she would marry you, with these mistaken ideas your marriage would be less than the full beauty and wonder of what God and the Scriptures indicate marriage should be. If you have been in contact with Christians who have given you this poor advice, I urge you not to listen to their bad advice and poor teaching concerning the Bible any longer. I say this even though I realize it may easily be that they are true brothers in Christ whom I would love in the Lord. But this does not mean that their teaching on this particular point is not wrong; and the desert into which it has led you (including false introspection) is a clear indication of the mistake of their teaching.

Finally I would say that none of this need destroy our love and [your] closeness in the Lord. You are still completely welcome to come here as a Farel House student, and as a matter of fact I would urge you to do so. Carolyn will not be here in Huémoz, and I would feel that it could easily be the best thing for you to return to us as a Farel House student *as soon as possible.*

Be assured of our love. We are sorry for this which has occurred and we pray that God will give you the richest of joy, as He is the healer when our hearts are wounded.

Mrs. Schaeffer and all of us in Huémoz send our love to you.

> With love in the Lamb,
> Francis A. Schaeffer

Divorce, Remarriage, and the Church

[Written in response to a sad and complicated situation involving a woman (Cindy) who, under pressure from her family, married a drug pusher after she had become pregnant by him. The marriage was really against Cindy's wishes, and she was able to go through with it only after drugging herself for the wedding. She became a Christian after her marriage, but soon became embittered by her husband's abuse of her and his failure to provide any support for her and the baby. At this point a young, unmarried minister (Mike) befriended Cindy and fell in love with her while she was still married to the pusher. Mike's friend (Randy) wrote to Dr. Schaeffer deeply concerned for his friend—that Mike might do what is right before God. Randy wrote to Dr. Schaeffer since Mike was a former L'Abri student, and because Randy had found little help in consulting with evangelical ministers in his area. At Randy's urgent request, then, Dr. Schaeffer wrote back directly to Mike.]

20th July, 1970   Chalet les Mélèzes
                            Huémoz sur Ollon, Switzerland

Dear Mike,

This morning I received a letter from Randy Davidson. Let me say at once that it was a good letter in every way.

In this letter, he told me about your present problem. As I think you know, it is my definite principle not to enter into other people's lives unless they ask me to, or unless I feel that it falls within the sphere of my responsibility of L'Abri or the International Church. Thus, I hesitate to write insofar as you have not written to me, but in considering the matter, I could not not write in the light of having been asked for my opinion [by Randy].

I am not in any way making a judgment as to this specific case. I would not wish to do so unless you, Mike, had a desire to write to me and tell me how it looks to you. This is not to say that Randy gave anything other than just a loving and gentle statement. I would not feel free to give advice until I had a clear picture in my mind as you personally see it.

The basic problem in all these things is the same: We must exhibit simultaneously the holiness of God and the love of God. Anything else than this simultaneous exhibition presents a caricature of our God to the world rather than showing him forth. We are in a day when evangelicals tend to let down the absolutes in the Word of God in doctrine and in life, and we must be careful not to contribute to this. On the other hand, we are in a day when other evangelicals are becoming more and more heartless, and we must be careful not to contribute to this as well. The problem is in being those who insist upon the absolutes of God and yet show forth beauty to the world, which is strangling for the need of both absolutes and beauty. These things are beyond us in our own strength, but not in His strength as we allow Him to bring forth His fruits through us in this sinful and ugly world and generation.

My own certainty as to the Biblical standard in regard to marriage and divorce and remarriage is the same as that held by the Reformers. I am sure that they understood the Bible correctly. This is that there might be divorce and remarriage on two grounds. The first is when one party has been sexually unfaithful. I believe that Matthew 5:32 makes this completely plain. Please notice that I am completely convinced that this gives not only the right of divorce, but also of remarriage.

The second reason is willful desertion. I think that this is made completely plain in 1 Corinthians 7:15. I feel that the Westminster Confession states the exegesis of this completely. The reference is, the Westminster Confession, sections XXIV, V.

If either of these two things is involved, I would fight for the person's right to be divorced and remarried—openly, before the church, without embarrassment and hindrance. If a person has been divorced prior to their becoming a Christian, and if the case is without remedy, then I think there must be special consideration. Notice, however, that it should be without remedy, and that an attempt should be made to pick up the pieces. If the pieces cannot be picked up, then I would officiate at a remarriage of this person, as the mistakes of the past are under the blood of the Lamb.

I must say honestly that I have a question in my mind whether an office-bearer of the church should do this. In short, I would perform such a marriage, but I am not sure that the man involved should then be an elder, at least until some time has passed. I realize that there is something a bit subjective in my feeling concerning this last statement—namely, about a person being divorced before he or she was a Christian. I would not wish [for my view on] this to bind anyone else, though it does fit into the Scriptures and into the marks given in the Scriptures of what an office-bearer in the church should be.

The thing I am totally certain of, however—and this is one of the things I would really fight for—is that in the case of unfaithfulness and willful desertion, the church should not only agree to divorce and remarry, but should publically insist on the right of the individual to do this as a Scriptural principle.

Do forgive me if I am interfering in something in which I have no place. I felt that I could not pass this letter by without saying what I did say once I had received it. I would say again, Mike, that Randy's letter could not have been more gentle.

I pray for Cindy and all the rest of you, and if I could be of any further help, please let me know. And, above all, make your decisions before the face of the Lord and His absolutes in the Scriptures. Do not be afraid of what the evangelical world says, as long as you are sure that you are right on the basis of the absolutes in the Scriptures. Do all in love, that no one might be injured, but that Christ might be glorified.

With much love to all of you,

In the Lamb,
Francis A. Schaeffer

Copy sent to Randy Davidson

Forgiveness for Past Sexual Sin and Marriage

[Joyce, who is an artist, writes to Dr. Schaeffer describing herself as "a twentieth century person" who affirmed relativism, a vague mysticism, and a very loose sexual morality, including affairs with several men. After accepting Christ, she went the opposite direction and did not even date for five years. Recently, however, she met a Christian man, and together they are seriously considering marriage. They both want to do only what is right before the Lord, but they are not sure how Joyce's past sexual sins relate to their desire to be married. Thus Joyce seeks Dr. Schaeffer's counsel concerning: what really constitutes marriage; whether she is married, in God's sight, to the first person with whom she had intercourse, even though she was not a Christian at the time; whether, being forgiven through the death of Christ, she is now free to marry. As a former L'Abri student, she had found a real understanding of God's love and forgiveness for her past. But she does not know how this relates to marriage since she had no plans for marriage and the question never came up while she was at L'Abri.]

5th November 1970   Chalet les Mélèzes
                      1861 Huémoz sur Ollon, Switzerland
Dear Joyce,
    Thank you for your letter of October 11. I am sorry not to have answered you before, but your letter came while Edith and I were away for vacation. I do hope that this delay does not make it difficult for you.
    I have read all you wrote with much care. My basic answer would be that insofar as the affairs you have had were prior to your salvation, certainly the blood of Christ has covered this—not only before God, but also before God's children. As far as any right or wrong is concerned, your friend and you should feel totally free in this matter [to marry].
    It is important to notice that Jesus Himself set forth this

view when He said to the self-righteous people of His day that the very prostitutes and tax-gatherers would go into the kingdom of God before those who considered themselves better because they had not committed these particular sins.

The Bible does not minimize sexual sin, but neither does it make it different from any other sin. I think it is very significant that in the sin lists in the writings of Paul, he very carefully breaks up the lists of the sins so that sometimes one sin is in the first place and sometimes another. This, I feel, is deliberate in the inspiration of the Holy Spirit, to indicate that one sin is not greater than another, and that all sins are forgiven by the blood of Christ. Thus, on the basis of right and wrong, your friend should not let this matter come into question any more than whatever particular sins he has committed and has brought under the blood.

Not in the area of right or wrong, but in the area of [his own] mentality, your friend should honestly face his own mind. He should realize that your sin of the past was completely covered by the blood of Christ when you accepted Christ as a Savior, and this should be so for all Christians and for him. On the other hand, he should be honest in facing another question—and that is that there not be any hindrance in your marriage because of these things [in the past]. Is he quite sure that you are indeed brothers and sisters in Christ, and that he will not at some later date raise this question with you again? In other words, coming on a Biblical basis to the knowledge that there is no wrong in this, will this knowledge be so profound with him that this matter will never be raised again as a hindrance between you in the years to come when you are married? And when, as in any marriage, problems arise?

Thus, I would say that there is no question of wrong in this, but that you must in this particular matter be totally open with each other as you consider together before the Lord whether the Lord means you to marry. Being fond of you as we are, we hope that you will be at rest in this matter and that the Lord will give you joy. . . .

We love you,

In the Lamb,
Francis A. Schaeffer

Marriage and Age

27th May 1971   Chalet les Mélèzes
                          1861 Huémoz sur Ollon, Switzerland

Dear Linda,

Thank you for your letter. . . . I am sorry not to have answered before, but Edith and I brought back a bad virus [from our recent trip to the L'Abri Conference in Tennessee], and being so tired it was very hard for us to throw it off. With the pressure of catching up on the work upon our return, and with the manuscripts of two books to work over, my correspondence has gradually drifted behind. I am sorry, though, that I didn't answer with at least a note before.

I read all you wrote with much interest and have been thinking of you ever since. In my loving care for you I would say two things. First, age in marriage just doesn't make any difference, and we mustn't let people make us feel as though it does make a difference. Love, like sexual maturity, is not a matter of age. On the other hand, I do think there is a danger—if a girl is older and has been of a very great and specific help to the man, that in the marriage he leans upon her more than should be the case for his good or for hers.

Thus, I would urge you to pray carefully, that you may be sure this is the Lord's leading for you. Be honest with yourself in knowing that it is easy for a woman to let her natural desires to be married creep into her decision. Of course, it is not wrong to desire to be married, but I have known some girls who so put this first that they have not listened carefully to the leading of the Lord. My experience is that it is hard for a woman to be objective at this point.

Thus, my word would be to go along gently. But if this is of the Lord, He will make it plain to you if you are really open before Him. Either way, I do pray that this boy [i.e., Linda's prospective husband] will able to be helped, and looking to the Lord that he will have all the joy of development and fulfillment which we as children of God through Christ should have.

We were touched by the conference as we were reminded once again of the wide spectrum of people over which the Lord is using L'Abri.

With warm personal greetings,

> In the Lamb,
> Francis A. Schaeffer

Adultery, Forgiveness and Reconciliation in Marriage

[To Matt, a married man with young children who had an affair with another married woman. The affair left a wake of destruction in the two families involved, and in the lives of many others. Matt's wife Ellen is open to reconciliation, but many deep wounds remain unhealed. Dr. Schaeffer writes first to correct a specific misunderstanding, but more generally to offer help and hope for forgiveness and reconciliation.]

December 21, 1971　　　　Chalet les Mélèzes
　　　　　　　　　　　　1861 Huémoz, Switzerland

Dear Matt,

Ever since I was in [your area] I have been wondering if there was some way I could reach you. When I was there, I was told that no one knew where you were. Now just yesterday I received a letter [from a friend of yours] saying that I could reach you through this address. I do want you to know that I have prayed for you constantly.

In this letter which I just received, it says that you had understood that I had said something to [one of our workers] which would indicate that I did not think you could be used by the Lord again. I want to assure you I don't think this is the case, and there must have been a misunderstanding somewhere along the line.

Of course, I do not need to tell you that the matter is certainly complicated, but happily the blood of Christ really can cleanse everything. It is wonderful that because Christ is God His death has infinite value and so can cover everything. It is a good thing that this is the case, or the Lord could not use any of us, for we are all sinners.

How the Lord could use you, of course, is between you and the Lord. There are always two sides to the matter. The one is our relationship to the Lord Himself, and the other concerns those we have hurt. At times it is easier for the Lord to use us in a different locality than in the place in which we have made our mistakes. I am not saying this is necessarily true in your case. But sometimes I have observed that it does work this way because, while the Lord forgives us, unhappily Satan can use our mistakes to throw up road-blocks among those that we are trying to help.

It would seem to me that the first step is for Ellen and you to get the pieces put back together. I am sure that it must be very difficult for you not to feel as though you are in Alice in Wonderland's upside-down world. However, I am sure that as you return to life within the structure of Scripture, under the leadership of the Spirit, the Lord can cause the two of you to find a way to serve the Lord and have fulfillment as well.

I wonder therefore if there isn't some way for Ellen and yourself to get alone somewhere for a while, without the children if possible—in order to get things worked through individually before the Lord, and then as a couple before the Lord.

We're jammed out to the doors, but if it would be possible

for you financially, I think it might be helpful if the two of you could come over to one of the pensions in the village and spend some weeks here. I do believe the Lord gave us a closeness when you were here both times, and I would hope that the Lord would use this place, as he has with a number of other couples, for a time of real healing. As I say, if you could be without the children, this I am sure would be best under the circumstances, and of course it would make it easier to stay in a pension.

Please do not fear to come, for we all have gone through our rough times though somewhat different from yours. But neither Edith nor I would feel that any of us have any right to thunder at each other. As brothers and sisters in Christ we do have the responsibility of letting the Bible speak to each other, but that is very different than feeling that we have anything to say as though *we* were somebody. As I have said, ever since I heard about this I've just prayed for you, and prayed for you, and I would be glad if we could be a help.

On the other hand, of course, there are all the other people who have been injured to think about—Ellen, the people who have been with you in the work, the other woman, her children and her husband. Each of these has in their own way been injured, and one must think of how each could be helped. A matter like this is far too complicated for any human being, but it is not too complicated for the infinite God.

The start of course is to acknowledge where we have been wrong, and indeed that we *have* been wrong. There is no other way to have our fellowship with the Lord restored. After that we must think what we can do to help the others we have injured. Surely the first step though is to trust God—and to trust Him specifically that, with your life in His hands, He will not just throw you by the wayside. But we must have a willingness to do whatever the Lord wants, and that would mean in your case a willingness to do something else in another place if that is really what the Lord wants. Again, I am not saying that this will be the case, but the willingness must be there on your part.

I have also been thinking about your physical illness and I am praying that the Lord will heal you from this.

I am so glad that yesterday I received this address telling how I might reach you. Really, it would be impossible to tell you how many times I've wanted to write, but I felt stymied because of what I was told—that people did not know where you are. I am so glad this is no longer the case. Incidentally, I am sending a copy of this letter to Ellen because, both from the Bible and from experience, I do feel strongly that if there is to be any solution, the first step is in relationship to the Lord, but the second step must be in relationship to Ellen and yourself trying to work out this matter together.

With love in the Lamb,
Francis A. Schaeffer

Race and Marriage and Parental Authority

[Written in response to a letter from Sandy, a twenty-one-year-old Christian girl who wishes to marry a black Christian man. Her parents say they will never give their consent, while his parents favor the marriage. Sandy has searched the Scriptures and can find no Biblical grounds for prohibiting interracial marriages. Sandy writes Dr. Schaeffer for a Biblical answer concerning children's obedience and at what age children are free from parental authority.]

13 June 1972   Chalet les Mélèzes
                      1861 Huémoz sur Ollon, Switzerland
Dear Sandy,

Thank you for your letter of June 2 which reached me this morning. I have read it very carefully, and I must say I am touched for you.

It would seem to me that the answer to your letter requires two parts. The first is what is right from the Bible's viewpoint in regard to obeying one's parents; and then the second is the law of love which in the Bible is also an absolute. As Christians we are called upon to exhibit the character of God, and this means the simultaneous exhibition of His holiness and His love.

I am really starting in a backwards way, but I would say first that, acting upon what I think is right and in accordance with the Scripture, you do have a responsibility of fulfilling the law of love in hurting your parents as little as possible.

Having said that, I think you are quite right that the Bible gives absolutely no command or even any indication that there is anything wrong with people of two different races marrying each other. There is only one rule in the Bible concerning the Christian and marriage. This is an absolute rule that the Christian must not marry anyone except a Christian. Thus, as I see it from the Biblical viewpoint, two Christians have a complete right to marry as long as they are sure before the Lord the other one is the one for them. As long as the other person is a Christian, they have a complete right to marry regardless of any question such as age difference, or social standing, or education, nationality, race, or language.

It is also true that we are to honor our parents. But this does not mean that they can bind us to do what we think is wrong before the Lord or to keep us from doing what is right. This is true even at an earlier age if the parents are commanding us to do something wrong, and here at L'Abri we have many young people come whose non-Christian parents would command them to do that which is wrong. But surely at the age of twenty-one you must make your own decision as to what is right before the Lord, and you must not feel guilty in your choice.

But two more things need to be said. First, you and your fiancé must face the fact realistically that there are special problems that come in marriages in which there are differences between the two people—whether these differences are vast differences of social position, differences of race, or nationality. My own three daughters married Christians from other nationalities. (They were not interracial marriages, but were of different nationalities.) They had to face the fact that the differences of customs put an added strain upon their marriages and that these *added* strains must be taken seriously because even in the best of marriages there are strains. Thus your fiancé and you must be absolutely sure that your marriage is right before the Lord, and that you love each other enough to bear the extra strains that will come to you and to your children as well.

The second thing I have already indicated, namely that you must be careful not to be sinful in ruthlessly walking on your parents beyond what is needed, if you do decide it is right to marry and you do marry. In short, in the midst of doing what can be right, you must not forget the law of love toward them. Thus you and your fiancé must show love to them, even if they refuse to come to the service or any other thing. This is right in itself, but also if you do not do this, you will leave wounds which cannot be healed later with your parents.

I would only ask you one thing if you use any of this letter with anyone—that you have them read the whole letter. Please give my warmest greetings to your fiancé.

In the Lamb,
Francis A. Schaeffer

Masturbation

19 July 1972   Chalet les Mélèzes
                                1861 Huémoz sur Ollon, Switzerland
Dear Jim:

I wish you were here to talk rather than trying to write. The Bible is a very practical and totally balanced book. It makes completely plain that there is only one proper way for the fulfillment of the sexual needs of men and women—that is the heterosexual one-man, one-woman relationship. Everything else is either wrong, or deficient, or both.

The Bible, therefore, speaks strongly against all adultery, fornication, and the practice of homosexuality. It does not, however, give a clear command against masturbation. I think, therefore, it does two things at once. It clearly shows that the only proper solution [for sexual practice] is in the one-man, one-woman relationship. And yet it does not give an explicit negative concerning masturbation, and thus puts it in a different category than adultery, fornication, and so on. I feel this is the reason that it is handled as it is in the Bible—that is, that in a certain way it does both things at once. One thing is certain though: if masturbation is wrong, then it may be forgiven, as any other mistake, when brought under the blood of Christ.

I am glad that my books have been helpful to you. . . . Under separate cover I will send you [the information you requested]. . . .

With greetings in the Lamb,
Francis A. Schaeffer

Dangers of a "Platonic Relationship"

[To Louise, who has become involved in a "platonic relationship" with a married man. The circumstances of the relationship can only be inferred in a sketchy way since Dr. Schaeffer destroyed Louise's letters out of concern for her privacy and protection. Although the relationship appears relatively "innocent," Schaeffer warns that it is never possible to have a merely platonic relationship between a man and a woman and that she and the man are headed for tragedy.]

31 August 1972   Chalet les Mélèzes
                                  1861 Huémoz, Switzerland
Dear Louise:

Thank you for writing so frankly and fully and I will answer you also frankly. This cannot be a long letter, but I thought you should have my advice at once.

Louise, there is nothing so subtle as the temptations in the man-woman relationship. No temptation sneaks up on us so quickly and unawares. From my long experience with men and women, I simply do not believe in the concept of platonic relationship. God made men and women when they were in love to be in bed together. And once we start out suddenly, as though we were going faster and faster on a train, the situation is simply too difficult to get off.

I feel sorry for this man, but I urge you to be careful both for your sake and for his sake not to get caught. I would not be alone with him at any time. And without being cruel, I would break off the tennis playing and I would not be in contact with him in writing. His wife or secretary or somebody will find the letters no matter how carefully you try to destroy them. And more important—it is simply wrong.

At certain points of most men's lives they suddenly think that their wives do not understand them, or that their wives are not responding sexually, or something of this nature. And then they raise their eyes and there is always a girl there whom they idealistically think will fulfill what they think is lacking in their wives. In the world this usually results in divorce or the acceptance of affairs on the part of both men and women. For the Christian there is no solution except terminating this kind of relationship gently but completely. Thus I urge you not to put anything in writing and not to receive writing from him.

You say that you do not feel love for him and I am thankful, for that will make it easier for you to do what needs to be done. But do not underestimate the strength of the man-woman relationship, and how quickly and unexpectedly—in spite of yourself—you can become involved. Almost inevitably it is the woman who is hurt more. The man may start the matter, but he can end it easier too when he is trapped. And the girl is usually left to bear the brunt of the tears and also what the people round about would say.

It is curious but people, including Christians, forgive men easier than they forgive women, even if the woman did not instigate the thing. I simply do not believe a friendship of this kind is possible without the man-woman thing becoming overwhelming. I would be careful to be friendly with the wife. But if possible, without it being obvious, I would go to church in my own car.

I have read both of your letters very carefully and the above really is my studied advice. I am destroying both of your letters.

I do pray for you in this time of spiritual wisdom on your part. Edith sends her love to you with my own.

> In the Lamb,
> Francis A. Schaeffer

Lesbian Relationships

[To a young girl, Donna, who is struggling with whether homosexuality really is wrong. She has a number of friends who openly practice lesbianism and who try to justify their practice on Christian grounds. Donna's friends, in fact, have encouraged her in this direction, particularly in her very close and loving friendship with Marsha. Donna writes that she only wants to find the truth, but that she is confused and afraid of what this would mean for her, especially in her relationship to Marsha. Some months ago Donna found "a new beginning" at L'Abri, and for the first time she feels like she is "actually living" and someone of worth. Marsha is making plans to come to L'Abri, though Donna writes that she is "going through hell" now.]

13 January 1973   Chalet les Mélèzes
                         1861 Huémoz sur Ollon, Switzerland

Dear Donna:

Thank you very much for your letter of January 1. This will not be a long letter, but I did want you to have an answer at once. I am so glad you wrote and told me how you are getting along. There is certainly no reason why you cannot be friends with Marsha, as long as you have the strength not to let the temptation become sin by your acting on it. If, on the other hand, you find that this is impossible, then you will have to put distance between yourself and her.

The people in San Francisco are really very very wrong in giving you very bad advice [in their approval of homosexual practice]. The Bible makes very very plain that homosexuality and lesbianism is wrong. This should be our main thing—that the Bible says so. But it is not the only reason, because my experience has taught me, in watching so many cases, that over a period of time the thing never works out right either. And therefore, as in everything else, what is right is also what is best for us—though that is not to say that at times it does not bring pain to do what is right.

I realize that there are homosexual churches now in California. But regardless of what they say about themselves, they are far from the teaching of the Bible and can only lead to fresh tears and sorrows, not only for the individuals involved but for the church as such.

I do pray for your friend. And if the Lord brings her here, I certainly hope that she will get much from it. As I said at the beginning of the letter, you can be friends, providing the temptation does not become sin in your acting upon it. But if you find this is not possible, do have the courage to put geographical space between you and her. Do continue to let me know how you are getting on.

With love in the Lamb,
Francis A. Schaeffer

Marriage Certificate and Ceremony

[Dr. Schaeffer writes here in response to a long detailed letter concerning what the Bible teaches on the marriage ceremony, the marriage certificate, and what specifically constitutes a marriage. Mrs. Wilson writes out of concern for the moral relativism she is encountering in her church, but feels inadequate in supporting her own views from the Bible.]

10 February 1973   Chalet les Mélèzes
                      1861 Huémoz sur Ollon, Switzerland

Dear Mrs. Wilson:

Thank you for your letter of January 12. Thank you too for the enclosed dollar. We will put it in our postage fund.

I am sorry that I cannot write you at length, but this has been an even more busy time than usual for us. The problem of time is always an acute one, but this is especially so now as we have just moved to a new home* and within a week must leave for five weeks of lectures in the States. However, I did not want to wait until I got back to answer you.

It is true that the Bible does not mention a marriage certificate, but the marriage ethic is quite clear. The Biblical position is that one man and one woman should be married, and that sexual relationships should be within this circle of one man and one woman. If there were no sin in the world, perhaps a marriage ceremony would not be necessary. But both the state and the church have emphasized a marriage ceremony because people cheat. Though there is no marriage ceremony commanded in the Old Testament, yet it is clear that there were weddings because Jesus attended a wedding. And it is clear in the New Testament that there is to be one man and one woman [in the marriage relationship]. Thus the emphasis in the Bible is totally clear on the one-man, one-woman relationship, and it is also clear that in the days of Jesus there was such a thing as a wedding ceremony.

I am really sorry I cannot answer you at greater length and do hope this is some help to you. I fear that many evangelicals are growing very lax in their sexual ethic. The tragedy is, on one hand, that many evangelicals are no longer as strong as they were about the Bible being the Word of God, and at the same time many of them are becoming relativistic in sexual matters and divorce.

With warm personal greetings
in the Lamb,
Francis A. Schaeffer

*In January of 1973 the Schaeffers moved out of Chalet les Mélèzes in Huémoz to Chesières, which was the next village about a mile further up the mountain. They still thought of Chalet les Mélèzes as the central chalet of L'Abri, however, and they continued to use Chalet les Mélèzes as the return address for their correspondence for a number of years. In 1981, they began to use Chalet le Chardonnet in Chesières as their return address.

Male-Female Roles and the Bible

[Anna writes from Finland in English, though this is not her first language. She writes nonetheless a carefully reasoned letter on the question of the Christian and Biblical attitude toward women. Anna feels that the Bible treats women in a demeaning way and that the church has always been insensitive and exploitative of women. The idea of God being her Father is particularly upsetting since her personal father was an alcoholic and cruel to her and her family. When she hears her minister refer to God as "Father," it brings her to tears. She cannot forgive her personal father or God, and she describes the general view of the church toward women as an "open wound." After having read and appreciated two of Dr. Schaeffer's books (in the Finnish translation), Anna writes for counsel about what she describes as a matter of life and death.]

14 December 1973   Chalet les Mélèzes
                         1861 Huémoz sur Ollon, Switzerland
Dear Anna:

Thank you for your letter of November 16. I do wish you were here so we could talk rather than trying to move along in these things through correspondence.

I do not really believe that the Bible puts woman in a position where she cannot be fulfilled. I can deeply sympathize with your own problem in the light of your personal father. We often find the same problem here—that is, that the word *father* in no way conjures up in the individual's mind what the Bible means by *father*. As a matter of fact, my wife has just finished writing an article in which she stresses the importance of Christian fathers showing forth the love as well as the holiness of God so that the word *father* will mean what it should mean to their children.

In any situation there must be form, and that is especially so in a fallen world. Thus the Bible says that God gives certain "offices" among men, in order that form might exist rather than chaos. Those who hold these offices are not intrinsically better in themselves. It is just that the office is needed so that chaos will be resisted.

The Bible gives various offices of this nature: the elders of the church, the state, parents, the employer-employee relationship, and the husband and wife relationship. The dilemma comes in that, because people are sinners, they tend to take these offices and make them into something that God did not mean them to be—namely, a despotism. This can be true in every single one of the relationships I mentioned above. None of us are perfect by any means. But as Christians we should in some poor measure return to the place of order, and yet at the same time totally resist the despotism that the world makes of these things. This is true, let us say, of the states and the employer-employee relationship. And it is equally true of the husband-wife relationship and the parent-child relationship.

In the parent-child relationship, the parent stands in the place of God, as it were, with the little baby, in having to do everything for it, including changing its diapers and making all its decisions for it. But a wise Christian parent will try to arrange the matter so that by the time the child reaches a certain age, instead of the relationship being like this: ◎ it is like this: ◯◯ . None of us do this perfectly, but it is possible to have a good parent-child relationship for a lifetime in this way.

The husband-wife relationship, of course, goes on for a lifetime. But in the relationship that Paul describes, the husband on his part is to love the wife as Christ loved the church. If this is carried out in even a poor fashion, the wife is not unfulfilled and does not cease to be a person, but is really fulfilled as a person. I must say that through the years I have worked consciously to try to see that my wife is fulfilled as a person with all her gifts.

I do not feel the Bible really does speak in any unkind way about the woman. Linguistically it has been true through the ages that in all languages the masculine form is used in reference to both the male and female. I see no reason why this should not be the case without the woman feeling injured— especially when one considers how utterly awkward it is to have to say "he and she" every time the whole human race is meant. Then, when the Biblical letters are written to the "brethren," there is no reason to think for a moment that this does not include everybody. I think you are perfectly right in saying that you should not be submissive because of your race or language or sex. I would agree with this. But I would also say, from experience with my own home and hundreds of others, that any time order is removed from the home there is chaos, because we live in a fallen world. This is equally true, as I see it, in the husband-wife relationship and in the parent-child relationship. . . .

I do not think we can totally draw conclusions [about God as Father] from what our fathers have been, even with the best of fathers. Rather, I think it works in the other direction— namely, that *human fathers* can find out what they should be as fathers in seeing what the Bible says *God is as a Father.* It is true that many fathers today love their car and other things more than their children, but this is because men are sinners, and it is equally true that mothers do the same today. And it is equally true that even children today are often completely self- ish in their relationship to their parents.

(There is no emphasis in the Bible that the woman is any more sinful than the man. This simply is not there.)

It is worth noticing that the Bible does not say that all men are head of all women any more than all children have to obey all grown-up people. It is only that within the structure that God has given within families, there is to be this relation- ship. It is my personal experience that when a husband and wife are Christians and work on this together, the balance can be worked out in such a way that the woman does not feel unfulfilled but rather fulfilled.

Toward the end of your letter you bring in the issue of Negroes. Of course you are totally right, and there certainly is nothing in the Bible that would teach anything except that all races are totally equal before God.

None of our families is perfect, but I do think that one of the things which the Lord uses here at L'Abri is the family relationships which we have here. People who come here often do see families which are, in some poor way, near to what the Bible holds out for a family to be.

I do hope this is helpful.

With warm personal greetings,
Francis A. Schaeffer

Homosexual Temptation and Practice

[To Mr. Wong, an Oriental Christian man. Mr. Wong writes that he only recently "confirmed" that he is a homosexual. He hates to think of himself as a homosexual and can't face the future. He wants to change, but despite his prayers and efforts he has not been able to do so. And he asks whether people are born as homosexuals or conditioned to become homosexuals. In light of the Bible's condemnation of homosexuality, Mr. Wong has resigned from teaching Sunday school.]

1 April 1974   Chalet les Mélèzes
                          1861 Huémoz sur Ollon, Switzerland

Dear Mr. Wong:

Thank you for your letter of March 14 which I have read with much care. I certainly would want to do anything I could to help.

It seems as though some homosexuals are born as homosexuals—what we might term technically homophiles—and some become homosexual through homosexual contacts. The important thing to understand is that the temptation toward homosexual practice is not sin as long as it is not practiced. In this case it is like heterosexual persons who are tempted. The temptation is not sin; it is a positive willing reaction that is sinful.

Many people, especially if they have become homosexual and not born so, can be helped and can go on to live normal sexual lives. However, some cannot. When it is not possible to get past this problem, then the person who is homosexual must live the way, let us say, a heterosexual girl who is not married must live—that is, there is a part of her life which remains unfulfilled. But I would point out that in this fallen world in which we live there are parts of each of our lives that are less than totally fulfilled. This does not mean that I do not recognize something of the suffering that it brings. But I would point out that in this fallen world this is not the only problem that leads to suffering.

If you feel homosexual temptations, but do not give in to them, I would see no reason why you should give up teaching your Sunday school class. The Bible gives us many warnings—for example that busybodies and talebearers also cannot inherit the kingdom—but it is pointing out that none of us can inherit the kingdom except on the basis of the finished work of Christ.

I do wish I could do something more to help you, for your letter touched me very much. I would urge you with all my heart not to fall into a practicing homosexual relationship with this man that you have recently met. Homosexual relationships never work well, for even if one has an "affair," rather than just random contacts, it never can fill the whole needs of a personal relationship.

I hope this is helpful, and if I can be of any further help, do let me know.

> With warm personal greetings,
> Francis A. Schaeffer

Race and Marriage

[Leanne, a young woman who will soon turn twenty, grew up on a farm. While away at college, she fell in love with Michael, a man from an Islamic background and a different race. Michael had given up Islam and became a Christian while at L'Abri some time ago. Leanne and Michael were considering marriage, but have encountered very strong opposition from her parents.]

19 July 1974   Chalet les Mélèzes
                            1861 Huémoz, Switzerland
Dear Leanne,

I have your letter of July 2nd and have read it very carefully and was very touched by it. I wish we had a chance to sit down and talk, but I will do the best I can in a letter.

It is not easy to answer you in the tension and pressure in

which you find yourself. And immediately I would say that no one but God Himself is wise enough or has the right to give you the final answer. I wish I could just say, "This is the way," but no human being has the right to do this for another. Each one of us who is God's child must find out for himself or herself what the Lord wants us to do—and especially in the case of crucial decisions such as the one in which you find yourself.

We love Michael very much; and there is no question as far as any one can read a human heart that he became a Christian when he was here with us. How much he has grown spiritually, I cannot be sure. When I saw him last, he assured me he was going on in a Christian walk, and I trust this is the case. However, everyone faces tremendous battles in our generation, and these men who have become Christians here out of the background of Islam will have an especially difficult road.

I am sure the Bible in no way forbids us to marry a person of another race. There is only one rule stated in the Scripture, and that is that the person we marry is a born-again Christian. Along with that, I would add that it is a matter of wisdom to marry a Christian on our own spiritual level, or above us, so that in the close confines of the marriage relationship they do not constantly pull us down.

As I say, I am sure that the Bible in no way at all says that it is wrong to marry a person of another race. However, one must have the wisdom to understand that as we differ from another one in marriage we will have tensions. This is not only true with a matter of race, but is true in differences in education, or social status, or differences of community, or any other large differences. None of these differences mean that we should not marry the other person. But it does mean that each of them is going to add a strain to the marriage relationship. Thus for each difference, such as the ones I have mentioned above, it is all the more crucial that the couple have a love for each other and a certainty that the Lord is leading which is strong enough to bear the weight of the tension that these differences bring. Whether Michael and you have this strength of love and certainty that the Lord is leading is indeed something you must deal with before God alone.

I can understand your parents' concern, and again the weight must fall on you to determine whether your going with Michael is indeed so clearly the Lord's will that you must follow it rather than your parents' and sister's desire. Of course, we should take into consideration our family's desire, but eventually this must not be the last word. The last word must be what the Lord wants us to do.

. . . [Though your marriage certainly could become a beautiful thing and be used of the Lord] this does not mean you should marry Michael without facing the fact that your differences of nationality and so on will indeed make tensions. Before you begin on this road, you must be certain enough before the face of the Lord to know that when these tensions come, both of you will stay close enough to the Lord to support each other in the midst of those pressures.

As I say, I have no way to judge Michael's spiritual life at this particular moment. If I did know where he was spiritually at the moment, perhaps I could give you a slightly more certain word. As it is, all I can say to you is that I pray for you, and really I became very fond of you in reading your letter. It is a good letter and an honest one. Thus, I do pray for you that you do not make a mistake, and I encourage you at the moment to take time to ask yourself two questions: first, whether your love is strong enough to bear the tensions which I have spoken about; second, whether you are sure that this is so clearly the Lord's will for your life that when these pressures come you will stand with certainty rather than waver.

I urge you to consider these things carefully with prayer. Our feelings of emotional love are important, but we must not allow them to completely overwhelm our thinking. Think it through before the Lord. And especially talk to Michael to be sure that his spiritual life is warm and that he is walking close to the Lord. As I say, I have every certainty that he is a child of God. But in your circumstances at the moment, it is important to you to have settled quite clearly and openly that he is not only a Christian, but that Christ is really first in his life and the Lord of his life. This is important for each one of us. But it is especially important in your case to be sure that you have a firm enough foundation to take a step that, to be quite honest, will undoubtedly lead to some things that are joyous and to some that will be pressures in the days to come.

My wife, Edith, sends her love to you with my own, and if I can be of further help do let me know. I do pray for you.

With love in the Lamb,
Francis A. Schaeffer

Breakdown and Healing in a Christian Marriage

September 6, 1974   Chalet les Mélèzes
                          1861 Huémoz, Switzerland

Dear Kristina,

Thank you for your letter of August 20th. I continue to be troubled over the fact that John and you are having problems. I just wish I could help more. I, too, wish you could come to L'Abri in the hopes that you could get help here, but as that does not seem to be possible, I do want you to know that I pray for you and really would do anything I could to help.

Kristina, as you know I feel very close to you, and you will remember some of the storms that I helped you get through when you were here. Do back off and try to quiet down and look at this objectively. I have learned something in life, including married life, that it is only the one who has been hurt that can bring healing. The other person cannot. It is the one who has been hurt who has to be willing to be hurt again to show love if there is to be hope that healing will come. This may sound paradoxical, but it is the way life is in our poor fallen world.

As Christians, John and you have married and you took your vows to be married forever. You must find some way to work it out. There is no such thing as a perfect marriage. The choice is not between a perfect marriage and breaking up. We all, including Edith and myself, must find some balance in accepting less than perfection and yet having some beauty.

With love in the Lamb,
Francis A. Schaeffer

Broken Marriage and Homosexual Practice

[After a number of years of marriage, Susan writes that her husband, Jim, has left her to seek a gay life-style. Susan believes that God did something very special in giving them a number of happy years of marriage together, but she grieves deeply now over their separation. Jim is being influenced by other gays and is trying to justify his homosexuality in Christian terms. He sees no hope of returning to Susan, though she is reluctant to think of divorce. Susan and Jim have been to L'Abri and are close to the Schaeffers.]

October 18, 1974   Chalet les Mélèzes
                                  1861 Huémoz, Switzerland
Dear Susan:

Thank you for your letter of October 1st. I had heard that Jim had left you and I was deeply moved, and now your letter has touched Edith and myself very very much indeed. I can just say that I am desperately sorry for you, but also for Jim himself. For this path he has taken can only lead to sorrow on his part. I am sure you know if we could do anything we would want to. Edith and I are going to be at _____ in December, and if Jim would be willing I would be glad to find some time to sit down and talk to him. I am sorry that Kevin was not a help to Jim. I must say I found Kevin difficult to be close to even though we tried. . . . I really feel that Kevin's wife has a hard road to walk.

This new gay movement, setting up Christian churches and so forth, is a horrible thing. It surely is one more mark that we are indeed living in the time of Sodom and Gomorrah in a very profound way.

Edith and I pray for you, that the Lord will give you his peace in the midst of this. It must be so hard for you. Biblically I feel that if he is practicing homosexuality, you do have a right to get a divorce, but this is not to say that you should do so. This you must determine before the Lord Himself. However, if the time comes that this is the thing you feel is right for you, then you must not feel guilty at all because I feel you have a complete right to do so if he is practicing homosexuality.

Let me say again that we are sorry. Edith sends her love to you along with my own.

In the Lamb,
Francis A. Schaeffer

Birth Control, Masturbation, Sexual Immorality, and Abortion

[Judy, who is in medical school, writes concerning the total lack of sexual morality which she is being taught. She became a Christian after having lived loosely, and now finds the kind of sexual perversion she is being taught to be very disturbing. Judy has read several of Dr. Schaeffer's books and writes for answers concerning a number of specific questions about sexual morality.]

25 October 1974   Chalet les Mélèzes
                             1861 Huémoz, Switzerland

Dear Judy,

Thank you for your letter of October 2. I read your letter with great care and was very interested in it. You are quite right, of course, that the modern view is that man is an animal and that there is no real value system in the area of sex. We have come to the place where what is, is right.

The Bible tells us that the sexual relationship is to be within the circle of marriage. Of course, if people have made mistakes they can be brought under the blood of Christ and we can be forgiven and have a fresh start. But the Biblical absolute is clear that all sex is to be in the man-woman relationship and within marriage.

Actually I think the Bible is silent about masturbation. The general rule is that sex is to be within marriage, and this would seem to put masturbation outside what is right. And yet the fact that the Bible is silent about it does seem to me to put it in a different category than heterosexual relationships outside of marriage, or homosexual or lesbian relationships which are clearly commanded against in Scripture.

I do not think the Bible is against birth control as such. As I see it, the Bible says that one result of the Fall was increased conception. [Since increased conception is a result of the Fall and therefore abnormal, the use of] birth control in offsetting conception would then be the same as [the use of] medicine [in treating disease which, of course, is another abnormal consequence of the Fall]. The difficulty is, of course, that in the relativistic world in which we live, birth control is then used not only in sexual relationships in marriage, but to make easy promiscuous sexual relationships. But this does not make birth control wrong in itself.

I feel that abortion is murder. . . . I do think that this is what the Bible would set forth. It is interesting that the people who are for abortion tend also to be for euthanasia. I think both spring from the fact that modern man does not feel that man is unique, and sees him only as a part of the continuum from the molecule onward. The Bible says, of course, that man is unique because he is made in the image of God.

I am so glad the books have been helpful to you, and I hope this is helpful.

> With warm personal greetings
> in the Lamb,
> Francis A. Schaeffer

Male-Female Roles—Order and Balance

[To Ms. Donna Nelson, a wife and mother of three. Ms. Nelson writes a carefully reasoned, articulate letter in which she takes issue with Dr. Schaeffer's views on the male-female relationship and his understanding of the Biblical teaching about order within the Christian home. Her main point is that Jesus sets us free from "sexist hang-ups" and that as Christians we need to have a proper attitude toward women. She believes this is emerging in the woman's movement, but she is unhappy not to find the church taking the lead in this area. She then encourages Schaeffer to take the lead himself through his own writing.]

October 26, 1974   Chalet les Mélèzes
                             1861 Huémoz, Switzerland

Dear Ms. Nelson:

Thank you for your letter of September 7th. I received it when I got home from lectures in England and America, and I read it with a great deal of interest.

I really did read it with much interest! There are many things in your letter that I would totally agree with. Most of all, there is no doubt about it that man has treated woman badly. However, this is, I think, because man is a sinner and therefore has used badly the structure that God gave. Of course it is not only that man has treated woman badly, but man has treated man badly, and woman has treated woman badly, and both men and women have treated children badly. As sinners since the Fall we do not do very well in any of the relationships of life.

As I see it, after the Fall God gave certain points of order so that the fallen world would not drift into chaos as it otherwise naturally would. These are the husband-wife relationship, the parent-child relationship, and the employer-employee relationship. All are stated in Ephesians as well as other places in Paul's writings. Then from other places in the New Testament two more such points may be added—namely, the church officer-church member relationship, and the state-citizen relationship.

The people involved in these relationships are not in a superior or lower position. It is simply that a certain set of people are given an "office." This is to give order in a fallen world, and for this office they are responsible as stewards. The Bible sets these things forth in couplets: For example, the wife is to obey the husband, but he on his part is to love her as Christ loves the Church; the children are to obey the parents, but the father is to be careful not to drive his children up the wall.

Being sinful, each of us likes to stress one side of the couplet and forget the other side—and surely husbands have done this with wives, and men with women in a more general way. But as I see it, God has given these points of order since the Fall, and if we are really going to live upon the basis of the Bible we must live within these.

Please note this: I would stress that this is not a question of men being superior to women in any way; rather it is a question of order within the husband-wife relationship—and even there, it seems to me, the husband's part is really more difficult than the wife's. For me to love my wife the way Christ loved the church is a tremendous responsibility.

I would say one thing further: within the circle of the husband-wife relationship as given in the Bible, it is the husband's responsibility to see that the wife has her opportunities of fulfillment. The stress should be on partnership, but always within the structure that God has given.

> With warm personal greetings
> in the Lamb,
> Francis A. Schaeffer

Being Single

February 15, 1978   Chalet les Mélèzes
                           1861 Huémoz, Switzerland

Dear Mr. Anderson:

Thank you for your letter [asking about ministry to single persons in the church]. . . .

Basically, I would begin with the fact that each person has his or her own call from the Lord, and this includes some to be married and some to be single. Neither calling is higher than the other, and we must not allow the older social pressures, especially of the girl feeling unsuccessful if she is unmarried, to influence our Christian thinking.

Certainly marriage is for most Christians since God made man male and female in the first place. On the other hand, the two outstanding figures of the New Testament—Christ Himself and the Apostle Paul—both were unmarried. Both Christ and the Apostle Paul, however, make it plain that just because *they* were unmarried, this *does not mean* that it is a higher calling to be unmarried. However, since they were unmarried, this certainly shows without a doubt that *it is not a lower calling* to be single.

In L'Abri we have both married and single workers, and all have their place and serve as equals. Each has their own contributions which the other could not make.

Thus, whether we are married or not we should be under the leadership of the Holy Spirit, and it is not a matter of better or less. Then, of course, whether married or single the next step is that we must look to the leading of the Lord to know where we should serve either as a couple or as a single person.

I trust this is helpful. With warm personal greetings,

In the Lamb,
Francis A. Schaeffer

Divorce and Remarriage (and Women Teaching in the Church)

[Written in response to specific questions from a deacon writing as an official representative of the deacons board in a local church.]

April 15, 1978   Chalet les Mélèzes
                                   1861 Huémoz, Switzerland

Dear Mr. Decker:

Thank you for your letter of March 16. Please pardon the haste of this letter, as I am very pressed as we are working on a new book and film, but I did want to answer you personally.

I believe that the New Testament sets forth two, and only two, reasons for divorce and remarriage. However, I do believe that in these two cases the person does have a right both to divorce and then to remarry. These two cases are based on Matthew 5:31, 32 and 1 Corinthians 7:15. Incidentally, the Westminster Confession very clearly sets forth this same position in the following words:

> "XXIV, 5 Adultery or fornication, committed after a contract, being detected before marriage, giveth just occasion to the innocent party to dissolve that contract (Matthew 1:18-20). In the case of adultery after marriage, it is lawful for the innocent party to sue out a divorce, and after the divorce to marry another (Matthew 5:31, 32), as if the offending party were dead."

> "XXIV, 5 . . . yet nothing but adultery or such willful desertion as can no way be remedied by the church or civil magistrate (1 Corinthians 7:15) is cause sufficient of dissolving the bond of marriage."

We must never forget what I think is the central problem today—namely, the scandalous way in which so much of the church which calls itself evangelical has accepted divorce for *any* reason. And this is happening not only among church members, but also among pastors and officers of the church. This, I think, is specifically related to the fact that increasingly the Bible is no longer held to be absolute among those who claim to be evangelicals. This, of course, is in direct contradiction of what the Bible claims for itself and what Christ Himself claimed the Bible to be. Thus, with the Bible weakened in authority, increasingly the Bible becomes a "rubber Bible" and is bent to the relativistic thinking and behavior of our own day. One aspect of this is surely the easy attitude taken toward divorce and remarriage. On the other hand, this does not, I believe, change what I wrote above about the limited cases where I feel the Bible does give us the right to divorce and remarry.

For the second question, I do not think there is anything in the Bible which would forbid a woman from teaching such a Sunday school class. I think what the Bible states clearly is that a woman should not be in the position of an elder in the local congregation. I do not think this should be extended into the situation of the Sunday school which you described. I do think, however, that the election of women in many churches as pastors and elders is also due to the weakening of the authority of the Bible. . . .

I trust this is helpful, and would ask you to pray for us as we very much need prayer, especially as we move further with the new book and film.

With warm personal greetings,

In the Lamb,
Francis A. Schaeffer

Homosexual Tendency, Healing and Practice

[For a college student (Tom) who is confused about his sexual identity and in near despair. Tom recently was influenced toward homosexuality by a television special on homosexuals and by the discovery that one of his uncles, who just returned to the area, is gay.]

January 3, 1979   Chalet les Mélèzes
1861 Huémoz, Switzerland

Dear Tom:

Thank you for your letter of December 23. This cannot be as long as I would wish it to be, as I have just gotten back from the United States where I have been for four months . . . and you can guess the correspondence I face. However, in reading your letter I did want to answer at once.

I read your letter with great care, and I am very sympathetic to your dilemma. In the middle of page 1 you say you are not a homosexual but everything short of one. I take this to mean that you do not practice homosexuality while you do share these problems as a person. I think as Christians we must face the problem thus:

1) The practice of homosexuality is always wrong. The Bible clearly says this, and it does not fit the creation ordinance concerning sex—which is the relationship of one man, one woman.

2) We live in an abnormal world, and there are many forms of abnormality. One of these is a tendency towards homosexuality. I think that more people today feel that they have this tendency than in the past because, in our relativistic culture, homosexuality is pushed more and more on people as an alternate life-style. However, there certainly are those in all ages who feel a pull in this direction.

3) There are many people that have gotten over this, and have been able to marry and live a satisfactory life. On the other hand, we must face the fact that it is so ingrained in some that they have to live a celibate life. We naturally feel sorrow for these people. But the man or woman so involved must not be caught in engulfing self-pity, because this position is really not harder in practice than the highly sexed woman that no one asks to marry. This does not minimize the problem, but just to keep it in perspective.

4) The Christian community should make a great differentiation between the homosexual or lesbian *tendency* and the *practice*. And the surrounding Christian community should give support to the person in whom homosexuality is one of the manifestations of our abnormal world, and [especially as such a person] stands against the practice.

I hope this is helpful. I notice that you ask if I know Kafka. Yes, he speaks very clearly of the hopelessness of the modern world.

Your last sentence spoke of coming to L'Abri. You must know, of course, whether this is the place for you, but in reading your letter I think you could get help here. I will put in a Farel House sheet just in case.

With warm personal greetings,

In the Lamb,

Francis A. Schaeffer

Premarital Sexual Relations and Temptation

[Written to a young Christian couple in Europe, Peter and Gretta, who wrote to Dr. Schaeffer "with tears" concerning their premarital sexual relations and the Lord's leading in their lives.]

January 21, 1980   Chalet les Mélèzes
                            1861 Huémoz, Switzerland

Dear Peter:

Thank you for your letter of January 6. It came only recently, and I am answering you as quickly as possible.

I read your letter with great care, and certainly we would do anything we could to help you. The struggle you and your girlfriend are facing is common to many Christians. It should not be, of course, but it is

The Bible makes plain that sexual intercourse should only be within the circle of marriage, and that the ideal is a one-man, one-woman relationship for a lifetime. Yet because we are still sinners even after we are Christians, often we get caught with our sexual drive. I do believe that the sexual drive is the second strongest in human beings. The first is the drive toward knowing the Creator. The second is the one we are talking about. The sad thing is that it is one of the most beautiful things of life, and yet, in a less than Biblical framework, it can be so destructive and filled with sorrow.

You did the right thing, of course, in together confessing to the Lord that what you have done is wrong. Yet, I am sure this does not remove the struggle entirely.

There is no reason why your past intercourse should hinder your present marrying. As a matter of fact, it is in the opposite direction. It is natural that love should move toward sexual intercourse, for that is the way God made us. Now that you have hurried the matter along, marriage, of course, would be the right direction.

Whether you should go to Bible school or not I have no idea. Maybe the Lord wants you to do that, or maybe He wants both of you to go on in the professions in which you have trained [in chemistry and as a nurse].

I do have a suggestion, and that is that together the two of you come to L'Abri. It would be important that you come together if possible. Here it would seem to me that you could get some of these things straightened out. You say you are under such pressure, and I understand that. But really you should be able to get this pressure removed as you look to the Lord and move in the right direction.

I will put in the Farel House sheet and also a travel sheet so you can reach us easily. I do hope you can come and that you can come soon. I don't promise, of course, that we could help you, but I think we could.

Please give my love to your girlfriend, and I send mine to you.

> In the Lamb,
> Francis A. Schaeffer

Lesbianism

[Two women, Kim and Becky, write to Dr. Schaeffer stating first that they are Christians, and second that they are lesbians. They have been affected deeply by the books of both Dr. and Mrs. Schaeffer, and especially by *The God Who Is There*, which brought Kim to a saving knowledge of Christ. Kim and Becky write saying that through study of God's Word and prayer God has changed many things in their lives, but not their sexual orientation. They write now to ask whether they would be welcome to come and study at L'Abri.]

August 4, 1980   Chalet le Chardonnet
                                  1885 Chesières, Switzerland

Dear Kim and Becky:

Thank you for your letter of June 17. I am sorry not to have been able to answer you before, but I just returned home from Mayo Clinic and found your letter among the mail waiting for me.

I wish we were sitting down over a cup of coffee to talk, and I hope that my thinking comes across to you even in a letter in a way that I would want it to.

You are welcome at L'Abri, and I and others would be very happy to have time to talk with you. If you come, we do trust that indeed it will be a time that you will find not only one of learning, but of warmth too.

I always talk very freely, for I think that is a part of Christian love, too, and I want to now. You should know that all of us in L'Abri are convinced after much thought—not abstractly either, for we have had many homosexual men and lesbians here—that the Bible does tell us that the Lord created male and female, from the beginning, to be the basis for sexual relationships. We feel that truly one cannot deal with the Bible's teachings fairly without coming to this conclusion. As I say, this has not come through merely cold consideration, but out of a very personal relationship with many who are wrestling with this question on a personal level.

However, the whole Bible makes a great distinction between temptation and practice. Surely the church has been desperately wrong in acting as though the homosexual and lesbian tendency is somehow in itself a worse tendency than, let us say, a tendency toward promiscuity in heterosexual relationships. I think the church has had this reaction all too often because it feels threatened and has not known how to handle the matter. We have not found this problem. And thus we feel that it is truly possible to say gently and yet clearly that this practice is not what God has created us for, and still have a relationship as brothers and sisters in Christ and also as friends.

You should know, though, that if you come we will urge you not to practice lesbianism, even though you may have a tendency toward it. To this end you would not live together while you are with us. You could talk to any of the staff about this with no reservations. But knowing what we teach from before the time you come, we would expect you not to use your time here as a forum to try to influence others who are not on the staff.

Understanding each other then, if you want to come, I would say, "Welcome."

With warm personal greetings,

In the Lamb,
Francis A. Schaeffer

Lesbianism (Continued)

[Dr. Schaeffer's letter of August 4 touched Kim and Becky "more than you can know"—especially, they write, since they are not used to being greeted as sisters in Christ. Kim and Becky do not see any way to come to L'Abri, but they want to continue corresponding with Dr. Schaeffer since his letter "opened up a floodgate of need." In their long and articulate letter, they tell first of their total commitment to Christ and to the Bible as the inerrant Word of God. They then unfold their story of how they began to practice lesbianism many years ago; how they had a ministry of spiritual and emotional healing in a gay church; how they were later driven out of the church; and how they came through a long struggle with poverty and despair. They write now for help and direction in their lives, trying to understand why this has happened to them, and hoping for a new ministry of service. They have begged God to show them if there is any sin in their lives, and are convinced that God has not shown their lesbian relationship to be sin and the source of their frustration and need. Thus, Kim and Becky write to Dr. Schaeffer "as a father in Christ," hoping that he can help them.]

August 28, 1980   Chalet le Chardonnet
                           1885 Chesières, Switzerland

Dear Kim and Becky:

Thank you for your letter of August 12. I am glad that my letter of August 4 was helpful to you.

Yes, a year and ten months ago I found I have lymphoma [cancer]. I was very ill at the time, though I did not realize it, and found it out just in the last couple days when we were finishing the film *Whatever Happened to the Human Race?* Since then I have been on chemotherapy and it has gone well, and I am thankful. I do think looking back over the past year and ten months, I have been able to do as much work as I have ever done, and I am thankful.

Your letter touched me very much and interested me a

great deal, including your experiences in the Metropolitan Community Church. I know of that work, of course. I felt along with you [over what happened to you at that church]. And I felt for you as well in thinking along with you through your other experiences—especially in the shift that has come to you in the last four years.

Of course, the doctrinal things you set forth are exactly what I believe. And it is upon this basis that we can consider the things which you wrote about last time . . . [without slipping into] the ebb and flow of modern relativism. In the modern flow of relativism, there is no real reason for any morals or law, principles or meaning. But since God has spoken to us [in His Word, we have] . . . knowledge that people cannot generate out of their own finiteness—that is, we have both knowledge and a base which finite man alone cannot have.

[If I did not have the absolute certainty that God has spoken, that God exists, and that He is the basis of all that is] . . . I would have no way to be honest and consistent and to know that all was not illusion. But happily this is not the case. God is there. This is the great antithesis, and this gives the possibility to be intellectually honest and to have a basis for life.

I do think intellectual honesty dictates that there is no middle ground here—though most people unknowingly are suspended in some sort of middle ground. They are caught between the reality of what surrounds them and the reality of themselves as human beings. . . . [Thus], their intellectual systems and life perspective do not fit reality, and they attempt [to resolve the inconsistencies by searching for] a middle ground.

At this point let me say that I am so thankful that you, Kim, became a Christian through the reading of *The God Who Is There.*

In your next-to-the-last paragraph you say, "We *know* that our love for each other is not the reason" why you are dealing with the shifts and problems which you face. I would like to make a distinction here. Certainly the problems are not a result

of your love for each other. That can be said with finality.
However, while I am not saying that your difficulties are a
direct result of the form your love has taken (only God can say
that), I would suggest that you consider this. There is a difference between loving each other and the physical relationship.
Whether your troubles come as a result of this [physical rela-
tionship] is for God to show you. But whether they do or not, it
would seem to me from the Bible that these two things—your
love for each other and the physical relationship—must not be
confused.

There is no reason that two men or two women should
not love each other with a deep and continuing love. This could
mean living together and having real fulfillment on a human
level. But that is not really the question here. Should the love of
two men or two women include the physical relationship?
From my last letter you know that I personally am quite certain
that the Bible gives a negative answer to this.

As I see it, the physical relationship, as an expression of
love, was given from creation to exist only between the male
and the female. If this is correct, as I am sure it is, than that
which is "normal" [i.e., normative or right] is not based upon
whether love is involved, but whether it [i.e., the action in-
volved] is in the original form [intended by God]. In other
words, it is "normal" [i.e., normative or right] only if the physical aspect of love is expressed in the male-female relationship.
It is less than God meant it to be if the physical aspect of love
enters into the love relationship otherwise.

Thus, remembering that I am not saying that your present
troubles are a result of this . . . I do think that it is less than a
Biblical position for you to be practicing a physical expression
of your care for each other. . . . Love between two human
beings wants a total sharing, and in the male-female relationship the physical should be one instrument of this. But . . . the
Bible makes plain that in other relationships of love the expression should not include the physical. [In my previous letter] . . .
I am sure I touched upon . . . the difference between homosex-

ual temptation and practice, etc., so I will not mention that again.

In this abnormal world, in which not everybody is called to marriage between men and women, it always gives me pleasure to see two men or two women fulfilling each other in friendship and love. But I do think the Bible makes plain that when the physical is brought in, we then pass out of that which God created the physical to be from the beginning.

I have no illusions that rethinking these things will be easy for you. But it is my hope that you would find it possible to do so. If this is so, my end hope is (and I have no illusion that it would not be difficult) that you would end in a close exchange of love without this being disruptive.

You wrote that you have begged God to show you that if there is something wrong at the root of your situation, that He would show you. I don't say it glibly, but I think He has shown you His way for your relationship in the Scripture itself, which you yourself accept.

Unhappily, I leave next week for a time at Mayo Clinic, to shoot a short bit of film, and then on to England for three seminars. I will not be back here until the middle of October. I will then be deep in a major writing program until toward the first of the year. However, if you write to reach me in October, I will do my best to answer, though it may be a little while before I could find time to do so with my writing. I am sure you will understand my problem here.

With greetings in the Lamb,
Francis A. Schaeffer

Sexual Relations Outside of Marriage

[Michelle writes Dr. Schaeffer a few months after having left L'Abri. Though she had been involved in Bible-believing churches in the past, Michelle's personal life had been a series of tragedies—including a series of marriages, divorces, and abortions. *Whatever Happened to the Human Race?* was being shown when she first came to L'Abri, and having had abortions herself, she was devastated by the film's message. She slipped a note to Dr. Schaeffer during the discussion of the film, met with him for personal counsel, and decided to stay on as a student for three months. During this time, Michelle found spiritual and emotional healing, and a real knowledge of God's presence and forgiveness. Upon returning home, however, Michelle has found her life to be a struggle. She has been unable to find a church which truly lives out the gospel in its teaching and fellowship. But she has also fallen back into a personal and sexual relationship with David, a friend from the past. Michelle writes that her heart goes out to David, who has many very sad personal problems. She knows that this sexual relationship is wrong, and she does not like what is happening in her life, but she feels helpless to change and without anyone to turn to.]

March 28, 1981   Chalet le Chardonnet
                                  1885 Chesières, Switzerland

Dear Michelle:

I am glad we were able to talk while you were here in Huémoz. And I am more glad that you were able to spend a full three months here at L'Abri. I am not surprised that after you got away from here you found the going hard. L'Abri is far from perfect and makes many, many mistakes. But the Lord has given us something of beauty here as well as truth, and unhappily it must be said that often churches do not have a combination of a clear doctrinal teaching and yet, at the same time, a practicing community. Certainly such churches do exist, but it also is true that often they are not easy to find.

It is a hard balance; but it also can be said that some people go away from L'Abri and look for perfection. I have a little sentence which is very helpful to me: In this fallen world, if one will accept only perfection or nothing, one always gets the nothing. That is because perfection does not exist in this fallen world—and certainly L'Abri is not perfect.

Thus we must try to find a balance: on one hand not demanding perfection; and yet, on the other hand, being sensitive when the activities of the church are only activities, and the turning of wheels, simply for activity's sake.

No, I will not say [that all you need to do is] "turn back to God"—at least not to that alone. From the very beginning God meant man and woman to have horizontal help from other people. Before God created Eve, Adam was in full communication with God, but God Himself says that Adam needed to have horizontal communication, and God created Eve. So, while turning to God is central, each of us does need to have Christian help. I would not want to have to stand alone even after all these years as a Christian.

I ache for you in regard to [your relationship with] the artist. From the Biblical viewpoint, you either should stop having intercourse together or get married. Maybe even more Biblically, if you have been having intercourse together, you are married and he should acknowledge it. If he wants you enough both as person and sexually, he must face the responsibility this carries with it. I understand your pity for his many problems, and I realize that it is easy to *say*, "Don't see him," but it is not easy to *do*. Yet, I would say gently to you that you cannot expect to stick your hand in the fire and not get burned. We are all sexual beings with varying degrees of strength of sexual drive. And if we put ourselves in a place of constant relationship, it is as natural as can be that we end up in intercourse. Thus, while I do not say it is easy, you must not wipe yourself out in doing what you know is wrong. I do not say this easily, for I realize that you are friends as well as the sexual thing, but you do have to face up to the reality of the place where you are. . . .

I do not know if this is at all helpful, but you do have a decision to make, and really, you are not going to be happy until you get it made. If it is absolutely impossible to find the Christian human relationships you need there in that geographical location, maybe you will have to make the radical decision to find another geographical place. I do not know if this is the way, I am just saying maybe.

Debbie is still having problems physically. I do wish you would pray for her.

Incidentally there is going to be a shorter L'Abri Conference in Urbana and a number of us are going to be there. . . . If there is any chance of your getting there, I would urge you to do so. And if you would remind me of who you are, we can start where this letter leaves off.

With warm personal greetings,

> In the Lamb,
> Francis A. Schaeffer

Making a Broken Marriage into a Thing of Beauty

[To Ian, an intelligent, gifted medical doctor and psychologist. Ian writes to Dr. Schaeffer as his "spiritual Daddy" concerning the deep distress in his personal life. Ian and his wife Elisabeth have been to L'Abri and love both Dr. and Mrs. Schaeffer dearly. Ian is also using Dr. Schaeffer's books with his psychiatric patients. Recently, however, Elisabeth was drawn into an adulterous relationship with one of Ian's friends. Elisabeth now sees this as a mistake and has tried to reestablish her relationship with her husband. Ian says that he still loves Elisabeth, and now she is pregnant—apparently with Ian's child. Ian, however, cannot get his wife's adultery out of his mind. He wonders if he can really trust her now and if he can ever get over the pain he has gone through.]

July 22, 1981   Chalet le Chardonnet
                             1885 Chesières, Switzerland

Dear Ian:

Thank you for your letter of July 13. I have read it with great care. You will know that although I am glad to hear from you, your letter has troubled me for your sake and for Elisabeth's.

I am glad to be a spiritual father to you as far as I can in trying to give advice. And both Elisabeth and you can be sure of my prayer for both of you since I know it must be difficult for both of you. My prayer will be that Elisabeth and you can get all the past things behind you and build that good and beautiful marriage that I do trust is the deep desire of both of you.

First it must be said that the blood of Christ can cleanse all things; there is nothing that the infinite value of His shed blood cannot care for. That is, though God is holy and demands absolute obedience in those things He has commanded in Scripture—things which are absolutes because they are rooted in God's character—yet Christ's death on the cross removes all the guilt regardless of what the sin is. On the other hand, sin does have consequences in our human relationships, and these too must be cared for. However, they *can* be cared for if there is love and "a beginning on both sides."

The beginning for Elisabeth must be to comprehend that if she had sexual relationships with [your friend] that this was sin, and she must not call it anything less. Modern psychology, of course, would try to explain things away, and modern psychology has no place for real moral guilt. But modern psychology is wrong at this point. When we do that which is contrary to the Law of God we are guilty, and the starting point is always to be willing to call sin, sin. On the other hand, sexual sin is no different from or greater than any other sin. And once it is brought under the work of Christ and His death on the cross, then the guilt is removed. Of course, the human results of that sin must also be cared for.

According to the Bible if one person in a marriage has sexual relationships with another person [outside of marriage], the "innocent party" in the marriage has a right at that point to get a divorce. Yet let me emphasize with great force: *That does not mean that he or she then should necessarily get a divorce.* I have seen marriages where either the man or the woman has sinned in this way, but after the matter has been cared for in love and compassion on both sides, they have actually had a better marriage than previously. It is not always this way, of course, but it can be this way.

On your side, Ian, when such things occur they are never completely on one side. We all can look back on our marriages and see that we have been lacking in what we should be toward the other person.

Now that you have been back together again, and I assume have had sexual intercourse again, you have reestablished your marriage since Elisabeth did what she did. Certainly now the two of you should be trying to rectify all that has happened—to build a marriage which will be beautiful, which will fulfill both of you, and which will be toward the glory of the Lord.

You, Ian, of course, have some forgiving to do. I understand that it is hard for you to get all this out of your mind, and difficult as you touch her body not to have all these other things come up before you to spoil your relationship. On the other hand, the place for you to start is to realize that we are all sinners, and that all of us have had those things which would condemn us forever in God's sight, were it not for the finished work of Christ on the cross. Thus none of us are standing on a pinnacle of purity looking at someone else far, far below. We are all sinners, though our sins may be very different one from the other.

In your letter you say that you love her so very much and that she is now pregnant. You did not say it, but I assume she is pregnant with your child. Assuming this is so, then you reestablished the marriage relationship with her when you had sexual intercourse. It is up to the two of you, looking to the Lord for help, to cause that marriage to grow—not only by both of you being legally pure from this time on, but also by building into your marriage the beauty of personal relationships which God created man and woman for in the first place.

You both will have to work at it. Working at it will mean having compassion for each other, and praying together (and separately) that you will have the grace of God to put this behind you, and to get on in your married life and in living. It will require both of you to consciously draw on the strength of Christ and not to depend just on yourselves.

I would say though, if Elisabeth is pregnant with your child, then what I have written above is not [just my opinion], but it seems to me it is imperative and that which is right before God, as well as that which is absolutely necessary for the child's sake. The child, after all, is half you as well as half Elisabeth.

If, when you first knew that Elisabeth had had sexual relationships with someone else, you had divorced her on that clear Biblical basis, that would have been one thing. But if you have now made her pregnant with your child, then certainly you must [do everything you possibly can] for a solution of beauty.

Edith sends her love to Elisabeth and to you along with my own. If I can be of further help do write again, and do know that Edith and I will be praying specifically for this matter with you and for you.

In the Lamb,
Francis A. Schaeffer

Divorce, Remarriage, and Church Officers

November 4, 1981   Chalet le Chardonnet
                          1885 Chesières, Switzerland
Dear Dorothy,

Thank you for your letter of September 29. I noticed that my secretary acknowledged it on October 13. However, I did want to answer you personally, and I am doing so as soon as I have returned from the States.

I read all you wrote with much interest and sympathy. I understand completely that of which you write as I have walked the same road.

Concerning [divorce, remarriage and] church officers, I would try to answer in two steps. First, easy divorce among "Bible-believing Christians" has become epidemic. To me, it is a real tragedy and further indication of the lowering views of Scripture. One finds Christian leaders getting un-Biblical divorce and going on as though it makes no difference. I do believe that the Westminster Confession is right in allowing Biblical divorce and remarriage for adultery and for unresolvable desertion. But I believe these are the only two Biblical grounds.

Our culture, of course, takes marriage very lightly, and the new "no-fault" divorce is the sign of the fact that the Christian memory in our culture is just about gone. Unhappily, this has infiltrated the church in many places. We should fight this with everything that is within us.

As I see it, however, this also means that if a person has one of these proper grounds for divorce, the church should then support him or her in their right for remarriage. In other words, while the church has the responsibility not to accept un-Biblical divorce, it then has the equal responsibility of supporting the person who is divorced on Biblical grounds. I think this is for everyone, including church officers. But then, of course, if a church officer gets an un-Biblical divorce, then certainly he should not be a church officer. In fact, I think—officer or not—there should be some form of discipline.

On the other hand, if they got such a divorce before they were Christian, it then seems to me that the blood of Christ can cleanse this sin, like every other sin. Also, if a person gets an un-Biblical divorce after he is a Christian and then truly *repents,* the church body would have to determine what the situation then was. But in such a case, to me, the person would have to wait a while before taking up an office—especially as we are surrounded by a culture that takes marriage so lightly.

Basically, then, these passages [1 Timothy 3:2; Titus 1:6] do not refer only to polygamy [as you asked in your letter]. . . .

I trust all this is helpful, and I would be very glad if you would pray for us as you can guess the battle is not an easy one for us.

> In the Lamb,
> Francis A. Schaeffer

Contraception (and Divorce)

May 30, 1982   Chalet le Chardonnet
                                     1885 Chesières, Switzerland

Dear Bonnie:

Thank you for your letter of May 6. I am so glad that *Art and the Bible* has meant so much to you. It is a real tragedy that much of the Bible-believing church has had such a poor view of spirituality. After we are Christians, the Lordship of Christ encompasses all of life, and each person must know what the Lord leads him to do. But there are no intrinsically higher callings.

The downplaying of the humanities and intellectual and cultural things has been a real tragedy for many individuals. But even more destructive is the fact that this poor emphasis has meant that we have lost the total culture to the secular humanist thinking. . . .

I wonder if you have read my new book, *A Christian Manifesto.* If you have not, I would urge you to get it and read it since it carries these ideas on into the areas of law and government.

I think that there is nothing in the Scripture which would in any way lead against the use of contraception. How many children a couple should have should be between them and God. I do feel that for a Christian couple to decide to have no children would be wrong—for this is a part of what God means it to mean to come together. I could well visualize some couples not wanting to cut off the number [of children they will have] by their own choice; and after they had had a certain number of children not using contraception, to let the Lord set the final number. On the other hand, this too [not using contraception] would be an individual decision before the Lord Himself.

Concerning divorce, I feel that it is an absolute scandal that un-Biblical divorce and remarriage is now so easily accepted even among church leaders. . . . [The very acceptance of un-Biblical reasons for divorce among Christians] simply means that the Christians are accepting the current world view of hedonism, and also morally and legally a concept of "no-fault" anything. . . .

With warm personal greetings,

In the Lamb,

Francis A. Schaeffer

Finding a Marriage Partner (and God's Leading in Life)

[To Marcus, a student at L'Abri two years earlier, concerning the Lord's leading and especially finding God's choice of a marriage partner.]

December 4, 1982   Chalet le Chardonnet

1885 Chesiéres, Switzerland

Dear Marcus:

Thank you for your letter of October 29. I was unable to answer it before now as my time in the United States was very busy and I had no secretarial help there. I did enjoy your letter. I was sorry, though, that things have not gone well for you.

I am sure that "God is not contradicting Himself in your life" [as you suggested in your letter]. We all have our struggles, and certainly we all have our imperfections. This is not to excuse our sin nor [condone] our imperfections. However, when the Bible is preached with clarity, the Holy Spirit will work in spite of our own weaknesses. Of course, if there is open defilement of the gospel evident in our own lives to others, this blocks the work of the Lord. However, it is always a gentle balance between looking to the Lord for His strength for our

lives so as not to hinder the gospel, and yet knowing that there
is no one preaching the gospel who is perfect. . . .

I am so glad that *True Spirituality* was a help to the
woman who came to you. It is so very true that nothing which
is really loving can be merely repeated as "pat answers." We
can help each other on Biblical principles, but the application
of them must then be personal—looking to the Lord for His
leading in them, and what they mean to us as individuals at our
time and place of life.

I do pray for you in your problem concerning finding the
right girl to marry. How to find the girl is, of course, beyond
any human advice. The important thing would be to be where
a possible girl that you could marry would be geographically.
We marry the people that we know and are in contact with.
They do not appear out of thin air as a genie out of a jar!

No, it is not true that virgins must marry virgins, the
semipure the semipure, and so on down the line. The blood of
Christ cleanses us—and as long as we are not living in deliberate sin, when we fail we can always bring our lives back under
the blood of Christ and be forgiven. You should deal fairly with
the girl, though, so that she would know who you truly are—so
she would marry the person that exists and not a romanticized
version.

[As to whether I would hypothetically allow you, knowing
your past, to marry one of my granddaughters], I would, of
course, want the best for my granddaughters, the way I did for
my daughters (and my son). But it is rather farfetched for me to
comment, as you asked, upon whom I would allow my granddaughters to marry in the light of the independency in our
family!

My advice would be to once more work through *True
Spirituality*, and really think through the implications as applied to you and your problem. . . .

Thank you for your words about what Edith and I have
meant to you; we are touched. On our part, we ask your prayer.
We have returned home very, very tired indeed. We very much

feel the need of the Lord's leading for rest, and also concerning what we should accept to do and what to which we must give a negative answer. As you can guess, this choice is often not easy.

Edith sends her warm greetings to you along with my own.

In the Lamb,
Francis A. Schaeffer

Roles in Marriage and the Biblical Balance

[Theresa writes that she comes from three generations of women who dominated their husbands. She tells how this has been detrimental to her own sense of security and fulfillment, but especially how this has had a destructive effect upon men in general and upon their ability to provide both spiritual and all other leadership in the home.]

May 4, 1983   Chalet le Chardonnet
                              1885 Chesiéres, Switzerland

Dear Theresa,

Thank you for your letter of April 15th. I am so glad that our books and L'Abri have been helpful to you. We are truly thankful for this. It was encouraging to me indeed to hear that *The Complete Works* were being used at the library where you work. I was touched that they were given in your mother's memory.

Of course, we must give all the encouragement we can to people, and we must show them very much the wonder and beauty of life. We can be thankful for all those children who have grown up in happy homes. The balance, of course, must always be kept between the wonder of God's creation and what it is in its fallen state. . . .

The balance in the home is always a very complicated thing. The Bible makes plain that there is to be a hierarchy in the home, with the man as the head of the home. Yet, of course, this does not mean that he should be a bully; and part of his responsibility as the head of the home is to see that the women (his wife and his girls) have the possibility of fulfillment.

Of course, it will also turn upon the character of the people involved. The balance between the husband and the wife will always be a delicate thing—with the man being the head of the home, and yet the woman having at times more ability of leadership in certain ways than the man has. On the other side, if the woman finds that she has these qualities of leadership, then she must be sensitive and ask the Lord's help to see that the balance in the home is not upset. If she fails to do this, she really is going against Scriptural teaching. But it does seem to me from what you say of your home that the balance has been lost somewhere along the way.

Over the many miles I could hardly say more than this. But the Scripture is clear that somehow in a Christian home the husband is to be the head of the home, yet giving the woman in the home a chance for full development of her talents. And, on the woman's part, if she has greater leadership ability in certain areas, by the grace of God she should learn to [lead] without disturbing the balance.

I do not know if all this is helpful, but I hope so.

With warm personal greetings,

In the Lamb,

Francis A. Schaeffer

Appendix
Notes on the Editing
and Acknowledgements

Although some of the material in this Appendix is covered in abbreviated form in the Introduction, the following comments have been added to provide a fuller explanation of how I have handled the editing of Francis Schaeffer's letters, and to acknowledge the many who have played an important part in the completion of the book.

From the beginning I have approached the editing of Dr. Schaeffer's letters with three objectives in mind, and with the goal of fulfilling these objectives without compromise or trade-off between them. These objectives are:

1. To select and edit the letters in a way that is in complete accord with Dr. Schaeffer's wishes.
2. To do this in a way that makes for a good book—that is, a book that will make an important contribution and be of real help to those who read it.
3. To do this in a way that will be honoring to the Lord and will ultimately give Him the glory.

The magnitude of the project was almost overwhelming, due alone to the fact that a total of 19,000 of Schaeffer's letters exist. I am deeply grateful, therefore, to Jim Ingram for his work in making the preliminary selection of 1,300 letters out of the original 19,000. Without his work, begun on a part-time basis in 1981 and continuing through spring of 1985, the final selection and editing would have been an impossible task. It should be noted that Jim is highly qualified and has an ideal background for doing the initial selection. He became a Christian by reading the Bible on his own (in much the same way that Schaeffer did); he has done graduate study in philosophy and other fields; he has a clear understanding of Schaeffer's thought and the work of L'Abri. In addition to this he married Gail Herzog, who was Schaeffer's personal secretary during most of the last decade of his life. Gail's part in the project— through her knowledge of the letters, her personal relationship with the Schaeffers, and her contribution to Jim's work—was extremely important. Both Jim and Gail are now L'Abri members and workers.

My approach was to immerse myself completely in the 1,300 preselected letters until I felt that I fully understood what I had to work with. At that point it became clear to me that the only effective way to handle the material was the way Dr. Schaeffer himself envisioned this. Schaeffer's main criteria (as sketched out to Jim Ingram) were as follows:

- The letters were not to focus on "Schaeffer the man" but on the subjects (i.e., topics and questions) being dealt with—not as an academic discussion, but as practical and often pastoral counsel, to the end that they may be of help to the people reading the book.
- The letters were to be arranged by *dates* and *subjects*, giving as wide a spread of dates as works well. Schaeffer recognized that the letters would reflect development and even some changes in his thinking over time, and he was willing to let these variations stand.
- The letters were originally grouped in thirty-four subject categories by Jim Ingram. Schaeffer's instructions were that the letters could be rearranged and grouped together under subjects according to what would work best.
- Schaeffer suggested that some letters could be combined if necessary, if the answers in some letters were too sketchy or incomplete.

• Concerning the use of personal names, Schaeffer was very concerned that the confidentiality of the person writing to him not be breached. None of the writers' original letters were to be included, Schaeffer stressed, since "the personal aspects should stop with me."

I have tried to fulfill these criteria faithfully in every respect, and indeed there was real wisdom in the way Schaeffer envisioned the organization of the book. Because of the breadth of material available, a broad topical approach, with letters spread over a wide range of dates, really was the only practical way. This also helps to reveal development and changes in Schaeffer's thought. For example we see his own spiritual growth unfolding in the first part, and we see how he then shares this with others in the second part. Again in the second part we see Schaeffer's early views on sickness and healing, and then how these views sustain him when he faces his own personal battle with cancer. In the third part, we see him change his views on divorce (beginning in 1957), and the careful consideration and development of his understanding concerning the Bible's teaching on homosexuality. Perhaps most interesting in part three, we see a shift in the *kind* of problems and questions that Schaeffer writes about—a shift, for example, from questions about premarital sexual relations to frequent questions about homosexuality, divorce, and marital infidelity. Thus we see a trend developing toward more extreme forms of moral disintegration and cultural breakdown. (This trend can be documented with greater certainty in the topical distribution of the 1,300 letter sample, and in the distribution of the 19,000 total letters.)

Concerning the personal names in the letters, I have used pseudonyms throughout. It seemed better to use pseudonyms, rather than just leave blanks, since names were necessary for the sake of clarity—especially where a number of people were mentioned, and to make apparent whether the people mentioned were men or women. It was also important to use names rather than just blanks, since a blank would undermine the personal aspect of the letters. The only exception to this is that actual names were used in reference to certain well-known people, such as classic Christian writers like Amy Carmichael, F. B. Meyer, G. Campbell Morgan and others, or in mentioning certain well-known liberal theologians such as Karl Barth and Emil Brunner. The personal identity of the people to whom Schaeffer wrote was also protected by eliminating or changing any details which might make it possible to identify the recipient. It should not be possible, therefore, to identify any of the people to whom Schaeffer wrote based on the information included in the book, and any resemblance to persons whom the reader may know is purely coincidental.

As much was retained of each letter as seemed best. Some extraneous material was dropped, but in most cases openings, closings, and personal comments were included since these help to give a sense of the personal interest which Schaeffer took in everyone to whom he wrote. Wherever material has been dropped, this has been indicated by an ellipsis as follows: three dots are used whenever something is omitted from the middle of a sentence. Four dots are used whenever something is omitted from the end of a sentence (thereby requiring a period to end the sentence); or wherever a sentence, a paragraph, or more, has been omitted.

Beyond this, the letters were selected and organized so as to make the best book possible. Again, Schaeffer's wishes were that the letters be topical, practical, helpful and personal; and that they not focus on "Schaeffer the man." Of course it would be impossible for the personality of Schaeffer *not* to come through in his own letters. "Schaeffer the man" is clearly present. But at the same time, I have tried to be careful not to aggrandize Schaeffer in any way and to be sure that the portrait which does emerge is painted with true colors, "warts and all." The goal throughout was to include those letters which will have the broadest appeal, that will be helpful to the most people, and that deal with subjects not covered extensively in his other writings. At the same time the letters are not intended to be a collection of "historical documents" which would unearth new revelations about Schaeffer's previously hidden personal life, nor are they intended to shed new light on past historical events. Similarly, no letters between Schaeffer and prominent persons have been included, even though we do have copies of many such letters written to a great many well-known Christian and other leaders. These letters were omitted because they did not fit the selection criteria.

Although Schaeffer suggested that letters could be combined (in order to make complete answers if some letters were too sketchy), I have followed this suggestion only in the case of a very few letters. On two occasions, however, a specific general topic is handled by assembling ten or twelve brief selections under one heading. The two instances of this may be found in: Part One, "Reality, Heresy, Eastern Religion, and Barth, 1956-1958"; and Part Two, "Salvation, Works and Grace, Eternal Security, and the Sacraments, 1972-1982."

I did find it necessary to add comments by way of introduction to many letters. (This is a common practice in books of collected letters. See for example: *The Letters of J. R. R. Tolkien*, edited by Humphrey Carpenter [Boston: Houghton, Mifflin, 1981], and *Selected Letters of Robert Frost*, edited by Lawrence Thompson [New York: Holt, Rinehart and Winston, 1964].) These introductions were often necessary in order to understand the situation or problems to which Schaeffer was responding, and so that the reader might be able to make an application to his or her own situation.

The 19,000 letters, out of which the 1,300 were preselected, all exist in the form of carbon copies. If Schaeffer's letter was a response to an earlier letter this was usually attached to the carbon; in some cases, however, the letter to which Schaeffer was responding was either destroyed for reasons of confidentiality, or the letter was simply lost. There are very few letters existing from before 1947. The main reason for this, of course, is that Schaeffer did not write many letters before then. Schaeffer also mentions, however, that he destroyed many of his old letters in 1955 (see Part One, letter of August 29, 1956). Though he does not say which letters were destroyed and why, it seems likely that these would have concerned the controversies and conflicts in which he had become embroiled. Although we may wish to know more about some area of Schaeffer's life or about the historical events he was a part of, we are limited by what remains and is available from his letters.

Most of Schaeffer's letters were dictated into a recording device and subsequently transcribed. (A few were dictated to a secretary and one was written first in long hand and typed later.) As a result the letters contained a variety of errors and problems of style. For example, the paragraphing and the sentence structure were often done in an arbitrary way; these have been corrected to conform to proper style. Some things were obvious errors in transcription—for example, when the word "past" was typed, when the word "passed" was intended. Errors such as these have also been corrected without any special indication in the text. Brackets were used within the letters in two cases—first, where the thought is made clearer by the inclusion of an assumed or unstated idea; second, where the meaning is not altogether clear and I have put in what in my judgment it seems like Schaeffer most likely intended. The letters also contained stylistic variations in how the salutations were punctuated, in references to dates, and in the way the return address was written. For the most part these were retained as they appeared in the original letters rather than being changed for consistency in style.

In some cases I did find it necessary to recast some sentences in order for them to be understandable. In general, however, the editing was kept to a minimum, and was less than would be the case for most manuscripts. Yet some editing was necessary throughout due to the limitations inherent in the dictation-transcription process. At the same time my goal always was to keep the editing to a minimum, to preserve Schaeffer's style, and to be sure that his ideas were communicated without any confusion as to what he intended. After having worked extensively with Schaeffer in the preparation of the manuscript for his last book I have confidence that the editing of the letters was handled in a way that he would have approved, and it was in response to Schaeffer's own wishes that I undertook the project.

One final editorial consideration concerns how Francis Schaeffer is referred to throughout the book. Schaeffer was known to a small circle of close friends as "Fran." Most other people, outside of his family and close friends, addressed him as "Dr. Schaeffer." Likewise when he was mentioned in books or articles he is usually cited as "Francis Schaeffer," "Dr. Schaeffer," or just "Schaeffer." This latter style has been used throughout the letters. Usually the first reference in a new section uses the full name with subsequent references abbreviated to "Dr. Schaeffer" and then simply "Schaeffer."

Finally, there are many people to whom I would like to express appreciation for their part in the preparation of this book. First, I would like to thank Edith Schaeffer for allowing me to have access to the letters, for her prayers on behalf of the whole project, and for her encouragement especially after she read an earlier draft of the manuscript. Likewise I would like to thank Franky Schaeffer for his part in putting the project together, and for his timely prodding to see that the book would eventually materialize. Again I would mention my great appreciation to Jim and Gail Ingram, without whom the preparation of the manuscript would have been an impossible task.

I am thankful also for criticism, advice, and encouragement—especially from my brother Jan Dennis and from Harold Fickett—which provided valuable help and direction at critical points. I would express my appreciation also to L. G. Parkhurst for his genuine concern for the project and for his contribution in the preparation of the chronology. Special thanks is in order to Denise Gill for her excellent work in typing the manuscript—often on very short notice, but always with a willing spirit and in a most dependable way. Also to Jon Dennis and Dan Bathje, thank you for days of work standing at the Xerox machine making copies of Dr. Schaeffer's carbons and the finished manuscript.

In addition to these, my wife Ebeth deserves more thanks than I can adequately express—for her daily encouragement and prayers, especially when the project really did seem impossible. I would also like to thank my six older children—Geoff, Jon, Jenay, Sasha, Rachel and Joshua—for lifting up their father to their Heavenly Father in prayer, and who now have seen another prayer truly answered. Similarly I would like to thank the many others who upheld this project in prayer. I was often aware of being in the midst of a very real spiritual battle— realizing first-hand that the real battle is in the unseen world, and can only be won through prayer and moment by moment dependence upon God for His strength and wisdom. I thank God for the reality of His presence through the battle, and for the help he provided in specific times and in specific ways. For without God's provision I am sure this could not have been completed.

Finally I am grateful to Dr. Schaeffer for the opportunity he gave me, through the editing of his letters, to learn something of what it means to live moment by moment in the reality and strength of the infinite-personal God who is there. Reading these letters and working with them day after day for many months already has had a tremendous impact upon my own spiritual life, as I pray it will have in the lives of many others.

Lane T. Dennis
August 1985